"So it really does matter that pastors in the what it means to truly be Wesleyan? Maddi contributors have given the church a treasure principles to today's pastors. A rare book indeed that is both academically worthy and practically relevant. As one who dares to accept being called a Wesleyan pastor, I deeply appreciate this gift and urge all pastors to read and consider the trailblazing example of our theological forefather."

Rev. Kevin M. Ulmet, D.Min, Pastor
First Church of the Nazarene, Nashville, Tennessee

"In this second volume of the Wesleyan Paradigm series, we have been invited into an engaging and needed conversation. The diverse and gifted writers guide us into fifteen dimensions of pastoral ministry. Their work is informed by Wesley's teaching and practice, yet speaks clearly into our current context. Pastors at all stages of life and ministry development will be challenged, reminded, and helped by this book as they engage in their pastoral practices."

Rev. Randy Craker, District Superintendent
Northwest District, Church of the Nazarene

"*Pastoral Practices* is a book that should be on the shelf of every pastor in the Wesleyan tradition. Its pages contain a balanced look at the life and ministry of a local pastor and are written by men and women who have practiced what they preach."

Dr. Stan A. Toler, General Superintendent
Church of the Nazarene

"Maddix and Leclerc continue to bring us excellent resources for the church. In this volume we are encouraged to recognize ways in which our theological perspective informs our ministerial practice. As Wesleyans our theology provides the framework for all of ministry, from the local church through the various levels of administration. At a time when varying Christian traditions are struggling with their identity, this book provides those within the Wesleyan tradition a road map to the future."

Rev. Dr. Carla Sunberg, Ph.D., Co-District Superintendent
East Ohio District, Church of the Nazarene

"The practice of ministry is the essential to making the gospel credible. As those who are a living embodiment of the kingdom, pastors and ministry leaders need well-planned and thoughtfully enacted practices that are more than mere 'busy work.' Here is a wealth of resources that are contemporary yet timeless. The authors have a wealth of experience, but also a skill at reflective interpretation of the role of ministry. This is worth reading, and applying!"

Rev. Jesse C. Middendorf, General Superintendent
Church of the Nazarene

PASTORAL PRACTICES

PASTORAL PRACTICES

a wesleyan paradigm

Mark A. Maddix
&
Diane Leclerc

Editors

BEACON HILL PRESS
OF KANSAS CITY

Printed in the
United States of America

Cover Design: J.R. Caines
Interior Design: Sharon Page

Library of Congress Cataloging-in-Publication Data

Pastoral practices : a Wesleyan paradigm / Diane Leclerc and Mark A. Maddix, editors.
    pages cm
    Includes bibliographical references.
    ISBN 978-0-8341-3009-8 (pbk.)
    1. Pastoral theology—Wesleyan Church. 2. Wesleyan Church—Doctrines. 3. Wesley, John, 1703-1791. I. Leclerc, Diane, 1963- II. Maddix, Mark A., 1965-
    BV4011.3.P3655 2013
    253.088'287—dc23
                                                          2013011958

10 9 8 7 6 5 4 3 2 1

For
Rev. Riley Laymon
and
Rev. Esther Bowen
very important pastors along our journeys

CONTENTS

Contributors
11

1. A Wesleyan Way to Pastor:
Wesleyan Theology as Pastoral Practice
Mark A. Maddix and Diane Leclerc
15

2. Ordained to Word: Preaching in the Wesleyan Spirit
Jeff Crosno
27

3. Ordained to Sacrament:
Wesleyan Theology as Sacramental Practice
Phil Hamner
38

4. Responsive to God:
Wesleyan Worship as a Means of Spiritually Forming Grace
Paul Willis
52

5. Representing God: Pastoral Care as a Wesleyan Essential
Jeren Rowell
63

6. Standing in the Gap:
Wesleyan Foundations for Pastoral Counseling
Glena Andrews
73

7. Filling the Bucket:
A Wesleyan Way to Care for Yourself and the Ones You Love
Michael Pitts
86

8. Leading with Basin and Towel:
Servant Leadership in a Wesleyan Framework
Ed Robinson
97

9. "Orienteering": Administration as Wesleyan Cooperation
Stan Rodes
108

10. *Via Salutis:* Discipleship on the Wesleyan Journey
Rondy Smith
119

11. Reaching the Least of These:
Hospitality as the Heart of Wesleyan Identity
Nell Becker Sweeden
129

12. The Divine Dance: Evangelism in a Wesleyan Matrix
Dana Hicks
139

13. Graceful Inclusion:
Special Needs as a Test of Wesleyan Ecclesiology
Joy Wisehart
149

14. Wesleyan Contextualization:
Pastoral Practices in a Multicultural World
Mario Zani and Carol Rotz
160

15. Case Study: Wesleyan Practical Theology at Work in the City
Jon Middendorf
169

Notes
179

CONTRIBUTORS

Glena Lynne Andrews, Ph.D., Professor of Psychology
Northwest Nazarene University

> Glena Andrews is a clinical psychologist with nearly thirty years of
> experience providing therapy and supervision for counselors. She has worked
> in a variety of settings including private practice, hospitals, VA medical
> centers, and community clinics. She also has consulted with churches on
> developing counseling ministries and with pastors who provide counseling
> for parishioners.

Rev. Jeff Crosno, D.Min., Pastor
Spokane Valley Church of the Nazarene, Spokane, Washington

> Jeff Crosno previously served large congregations in the Kansas City,
> Portland, Pasadena, and Chicago metro areas and has earned doctorates
> from Nazarene Theological Seminary and Princeton Theological Seminary.

Rev. Philip R. Hamner, Ph.D. (Candidate), Pastor
Overland Park, Kansas, Church of the Nazarene

> Phil Hamner has been engaged in pastoral ministry for twenty-three years.
> He has pastored churches in Texas, Missouri, Indiana, and Kansas. In
> his current assignment he is actively involved in cross-cultural ministry
> predominantly among the Chinese community.

Rev. Dana Hicks, D.Min., Pastor
Real Life Church of the Nazarene, Nampa, Idaho

> Dana Hicks is lead pastor of Real Life Church in Nampa, Idaho, and
> an adjunct professor of Missional Leadership at Northwest Nazarene
> University. Before his current assignment, he was the founding pastor
> of Beginnings Church in Tucson, Arizona, and the lead pastor of Grays
> Harbor Church of the Nazarene in Hoquiam, Washington.

Rev. Diane Leclerc, Ph.D., Professor of Historical Theology
Northwest Nazarene University

Diane Leclerc has published many articles and four books, including *Discovering Christian Holiness: The Heart of Wesleyan Holiness Theology* (2010) and *Spiritual Formation: A Wesleyan Paradigm*, with Mark Maddix (2011). She has served as president of the Wesleyan Theological Society and is a member of the Wesleyan-Holiness Women Clergy Society. She pastored a Nazarene congregation in Maine and served as the first pastor of a new church plant in Boise, Idaho. She is married and has one teenage son.

Rev. Mark A. Maddix, Ph.D., Professor of Practical Theology and Christian Discipleship
Dean of the School of Theology and Christian Ministries
Northwest Nazarene University

Mark Maddix has published many articles and coauthored three books, including *Discovering Discipleship: Dynamics of Christian Education* (2010) and *Spiritual Formation: A Wesleyan Paradigm* (2011). He also currently serves as the president of the North American Professors of Christian Education (NAPCE). Mark is a frequent speaker on topics of Christian discipleship, spiritual formation, and online education. He is married to his wife, Sherri. They have two grown children, Adrienne Maddix Meier and Nathan Maddix.

Rev. Jon Middendorf, M.A., Pastor
First Church of the Nazarene, Oklahoma City, Oklahoma

Jon Middendorf has served in his current ministry position for three decades, beginning as youth pastor and as senior pastor since 2007. His best days are spent with his family, making memories and a bit of trouble. He is married to his wife, Kelly. They have two boys, Taylor and Drew.

Rev. Michael A. Pitts, Ph.D., Associate Professor of Counselor Education
Northwest Nazarene University

Michael Pitts has served the church in a variety of roles, as associate and senior pastor, Church of the Nazarene International Headquarters, vice president for Spiritual Development and university chaplain at Point Loma Nazarene University, and currently as associate professor of Counselor Education at Northwest Nazarene University. He is an ordained elder in the Church of the Nazarene and a licensed counselor in the state of Idaho working with couples and individuals.

Rev. Ed Robinson, Ph.D., Professor of Practical Theology
Director of the Office of Leadership Studies and Servant Leadership
Northwest Nazarene University

Ed Robinson has been engaged in pastoral leadership, theological education, and Christian higher education for the past thirty-five years. Before coming to Northwest Nazarene University in 2011, Ed served for twenty-five years as dean of the faculty and professor at Nazarene Theological Seminary in Kansas City, Missouri, and president of MidAmerica Nazarene University in Olathe, Kansas.

Rev. Stan Rodes, Ph.D., Assistant District Superintendent
Intermountain District, Church of the Nazarene

Stan Rodes has served in pastoral ministry for almost twenty-five years in churches ranging in size from forty to four hundred. He has served as a curriculum writer for the Church of the Nazarene and as an adjunct professor at Northwest Nazarene University and holds a postgraduate degree in historical theology (Wesley Studies) from The University of Manchester (Nazarene Theological College), Manchester, England.

Rev. Carol Rotz, D. Litt. et Phil., Adjunct Professor
Northwest Nazarene University

Carol Rotz served in education as a missionary for the Church of the Nazarene in South Africa, Kenya, and Papua New Guinea. She retired from Northwest Nazarene University where she taught New Testament and was chair of the Department of Religion.

Rev. Jeren Rowell, Ed.D., District Superintendent
Kansas City District, Church of the Nazarene

Jeren Rowell, prior to election to the superintendency, served twenty-five years in pastoral ministry including fourteen years as pastor of the Shawnee Church of the Nazarene, Shawnee, Kansas.

Rev. Rondy M. Smith, Ed.D., Community Life Pastor
Hermitage Church of the Nazarene, Hermitage, Tennessee

Rondy Smith serves as Community Life pastor of the Hermitage congregation in the Nashville, Tennessee. Her responsibilities include Discipleship, Group Life, and Ministry Development for adults.

Rev. Nell Becker Sweeden, Ph.D., Professor of Wesleyan Theology
George Fox Evangelical Seminary

Nell Sweeden has directed the international program development for
Nazarene Compassionate Ministries. She engages in preaching, teaching,
and writing curriculum to assist in mobilizing local churches toward
compassionate outreach. She, along with her husband, Josh Sweeden, has
recently joined the George Fox Evangelical Seminary faculty.

Rev. Joy Wisehart, M.Div., Pastor to Families and Spiritual Formation
South Lake Church of the Nazarene, Crown Point, Indiana

Joy, and her husband, Lenny, were evangelists in the Church of the
Nazarene for seventeen years. They have pastored in Iowa and currently
pastor in Indiana. Joy is a frequent speaker for retreats and is an adjunct
professor for Indiana Wesleyan University.

Rev. Paul D. Willis, M.Div., Pastor
Generations Church, Farmville, Virginia

Paul Willis is a pastor and theologian interested in missional ecclesiology,
postmodern and relational modes of thought within the Wesleyan-Holiness
tradition. He is particularly interested in how each of these areas intersects
with and supports the planting and development of faith communities.

Rev. Mario J. Zani, D. Min., Latino Ministry Coordinator
Oregon-Pacific District Church of the Nazarene

Mario Zani serves as the Latino Ministry coordinator and church planter
on the Oregon-Pacific District and is a former professor of missions at
Nazarene Theological Seminary.

one

A WESLEYAN WAY TO PASTOR
WESLEYAN THEOLOGY AS PASTORAL PRACTICE

~~

Mark A. Maddix and Diane Leclerc

It is widely recognized that John Wesley's theology was not written in any sort of systematic form. Indeed, books such as Randy Maddox's *Responsible Grace* are gifts to theologians and pastors who want to investigate Wesley's theology systematically.[1] What Maddox and others have done is to take Wesley's entire corpus—which consists of journals, sermons, letters, and topical treatises—and glean from them what Wesley thought about each systematic category (e.g., Christology, pneumatology, soteriology, etc.). But what we must not forget when we read these extremely helpful summations of Wesley's theology is that Wesley's writings, almost *all* of them, are at least practical, if not indeed *pastoral* works. He had a pastor's heart.

Pastoral Theology

Despite his Oxford education and his knowledge in a wide variety of topics, in what we call the liberal arts, his aims were pastoral (even before Aldersgate, indeed even at Oxford!). By pastoral, we mean a deep passion for people that acts so that they might be nourished (sometimes literally) and nurtured in the faith, no matter what point they are on along the *via salutis*. We also mean that Wesley, certainly later on in the

Methodist revival, was deeply concerned to educate and direct pastors and preachers, society and band leaders in the spiritual care of people.

Wesley as Pastor

Wesley pastored people. For example, he certainly models pastoral characteristics in his own preaching and particularly in his *letter writing*. Wesley wrote over three thousand letters. It is quite clear from Wesley's letters that he was committed to the principle that letters should be "as near approaching to familiar conversation as possible."[2] He often, in fact, made reference to the last personal meeting, most often pastoral in nature, he had had with his correspondent and incited her or him to use the same degree of confessional openness on the written page.[3] The letters are a method of pastoring his Methodists for Wesley, since he was not fixed to one congregational context. Their content reveals his pastoral disposition.

There was a marked increase in the number of letters written by Wesley over the course of his lifetime. This can be accounted for in many ways, but the expansion of Methodism itself certainly served as the primary catalyst.[4] Baker affirms that "the rapid growth of Methodism, combining with his own inner urge to maintain personal oversight of its multitudinous ramifications and their attendant problems, necessarily entailed a steady increase in the number of letters which he received, from scores to hundreds every year, and even to many hundreds."[5] His need for control over the rapidly expanding movement drives his correspondence practices. He was especially in touch with his leaders and his lay preachers. In light of the number of letters he welcomed, it is astounding that Wesley seems to have abided by one of his own epistolary principles: "It is a rule with me to answer every letter I receive."[6]

Wesley received and answered over eight hundred letters to women.[7] It can be argued that while Wesley could still exhibit his tendencies toward expediency, his letters to women display an intensity of attention plainly lacking in his more administrative correspondence with his male preachers. They also evidence a deeper intricacy of style that enhances the differences in content.[8] Even in his intimate correspondence with his brother Charles one still sees Wesley the leader, the administrator, the champion of his own ideas![9] But in the letters he penned to women, a different side of Wesley surfaces, perhaps a side that better reflects the persona known to his followers in their actual encounters with him.[10] To some women Wesley wrote only one or two letters in response to some specific question. With several others, he carried on correspondence for over twenty years.[11]

In his letters to women we see him at his best, as a pastor and spiritual guide. Overall, the letters to women offer a different picture of John Wesley than the "concise, accurate, forcible, and clear"[12] administrator of a movement. The letters reveal an intensity of personality only deepened by the contours and context of a clearly pastoral relationality. In sum, we see Wesley as a true pastor to his people.

Wesley on Pastoring

Wesley did reflect more broadly on pastoral ministry, even while acting as a personal pastor to hundreds. The most explicit text on these matters is certainly his famous "Address to Clergy" written in 1754. Its audience included his own Methodist leaders, but interestingly in this address Wesley continues to try to affect Anglican clergy, despite his growing distance from them. He begins, "Let it not be imputed to forwardness, vanity, or presumption, that one who is of little esteem in the Church takes upon him thus to address a body of people, to many of whom he owes the highest reverence. I owe a still higher regard to Him who I believe requires this at my hands."[13] The following is an outlined summary of this treatise.

Pastors ought to be:

1. Overseers of the church who "naturally" display:
   a. Good understanding, clear apprehension, sound judgment, and capacity for reasoning

    b. Readiness of thought in order to answer any question

    c. Good memory

2. Persons who acquire (learn) the following:

    a. Knowledge of the office of minister

    b. Knowledge of the Scriptures

    c. Knowledge of the original language of Scripture

    d. Knowledge of world history

    e. Knowledge of the sciences

    f. Knowledge of the early church writers

    g. Knowledge of the social sciences

    h. Common sense

    i. Decorum in social spaces

3. Persons with spiritual dispositions based on God's grace:

    a. Intention to save souls

    b. Love for God and neighbor, even beyond nonclergy Christians

    c. Desire to be an example to the flock, in abstaining from evil

    d. Pure intentions for becoming a minister, free from greed for money or power

    e. An understanding of the sacredness of the office of priest—spiritual mediator

    f. Integrity in one's private life

Wesley believed that persons called to ministry must have certain natural abilities, be able to learn a wide variety of information, but most importantly, be receptive to the transforming grace of God that changes our dispositions and purifies our reasons for being pastors. Wesley had great expectations of the pastors under his leadership.[14] But nothing has yet been said that makes Wesley's way of ministering particularly Wesleyan! And so we now come to the premise of this book.

A Wesleyan Paradigm

The title of this book implies something important. It implies that pastoral practices do not form themselves in a theological vacuum! Or in other words, let's ask it this way: does the way we minister have anything to do with our Wesleyan identity? We believe it does. We believe that a pastor from a Wesleyan theological perspective will understand his or her pastoral identity in particular ways; that he or she will see the very purpose of pastoring in direct correspondence with the essence of Wesley's holistic vision; and that the very practices he or she will perform will be intentional in their faithfulness to a Wesleyan identity and vision. In other words, we believe that Wesleyan theology influences the following:

- **Pastoral Personality**—God has created each person to uniquely express the *imago Dei*. This is true of pastors as well. We are not advocating in this book that we all look the same, act the same, or pastor the same. But we do believe that being a pastor in the Wesleyan tradition primarily affirms that we are called to embody the God of love. This Wesleyan vision, indeed the very experience of perfect love, is to be the deepest affection in a pastor's heart. It is to form a pastor's character, influence a pastor's deepest desire, and empower the pastor's ability to re-present Christ. In the words of Wesley, love is to become our inner *disposition*—what we might call personality today.

- **Pastoral Purpose**—God's intention for all humanity is its sanctification. Before the very foundation of the world, God called us to be a holy people. The whole purpose of the church from a Wesleyan perspective, and the pastor who serves it, is to help people reach their full, holistic potential and to mature in the stature of Christ. It is to bring persons into the love of God, and that continually, so that they might then go out as incarnational witnesses to the world, indeed, partners in God's transformation of the world.

- **Pastoral Practices**—God has purposed that persons and communities be "shepherded" by one who is able to devote his or her life to such a high calling. Wesley cherished the priesthood, even while allowing his laity to preach. One of the primary reasons that Wesley allowed the Methodist Church in America to ordain its own pastors was because he believed America needed qualified priests to oversee the ministerial office, particularly to serve the sacraments. With the same kind of reverence, we continue to believe that while everyone in the church is called to minister in the ways he or she is gifted and enabled as members of the body, God continues to call and equip those ordained for pastoral ministry. It is thus with a unique, single-minded intentionality that a pastor pastors. More than that, we believe that Wesleyan theology is intricately knitted into the fabric of what pastors do, and that it provides unique paradigm for ministry.

Wesleyan Praxis

Let's reiterate some basics here. Wesley was first and foremost a practical theologian and he recognized the importance of the relationship of theology with the practice of ministry. Wesley resisted the division between theology and practice. According to Thomas Langford, "Wesley did not construct a theological theory which he applied to all situations; nor did he become a practitioner who undertakes application without allowing the utilization to affect its theoretical substructure. Wesley struggled to hold divergent dimensions in tight relation: emphasizing both, he allowed each to influence the other."[15] Wesley's *theology* is primarily based on a praxis approach, the integration of theology and practice. Wesley's *practice* is undergirded with his theology. Wesley's *praxis* approach is theology expressed through the practice of ministry such as sermons, liturgies, prayers, Bible study aids, hymns, essays, devotional materials, and journals. Theology serves the church. Again, Wesley's theology is by nature practical, as defined by whatever agrees with right belief (orthodoxy), right practice (orthopraxis), and the genuine experience of the presence of God (orthopathy). Practical theology is always concerned with and focused on *the renewal in the image of God (Christlikeness)*, which is the soteriological focus of Wesleyan theology. Soteriology by nature is practical and not speculative.

Wesley's practical theology thus recognizes the primacy of praxis. This primacy assumes that theological reflection must always be related back to praxis through such practices as constructing sermons, liturgies, shepherding the flock, and evangelism. The following are key aspects of a uniquely Wesleyan practical theology[16] and key themes at the heart of pastoral ministry.

First, practical theology should be transformative. Since humans are diseased and sinful, the goal of theology is to reform and heal humans. Wesley was primarily concerned with making Christians truly Christian; thus one criterion for assessing theology would be whether it resulted in transforming persons into Christians living Christianly in the world[17] (or in perhaps more familiar words: we are to Christianize Christianity). Franz Hildebrandt agrees by stating, "The meaning of 'practice' for Wesley is precisely parallel to the meaning of scriptural Christianity. Practice is simply and plainly enforcement of Christianity."[18] Wesley had very little interest in theology for its own sake. Rather, theology was for the purpose of transforming personal life and social relations. This *is* his "practical divinity."[19] This must be the primary objective of all ministry endeavors—to see human persons reconciled to God and renewed in nature. Wesley's focus on the transformation of human persons in the context of community provides helpful criteria to evaluate the effectiveness of contemporary ministry practices.

Second, practical theology should be holistic. Practical theology is concerned with the development of the "whole" person: the mind, the will, and affections.[20] Underlying this characteristic is the conviction that what ultimately unites *orthodoxy* (mind) and *orthopraxis* (will and actions) are right affections (*orthopathos*). Wesley was very insistent that good theology understands human affections as the heart of the Christian life, as the true motivator of all we do. Too often, however, we have tried to produce right thinking, and right behavior, and have neglected the centrality of "heart religion" for Wesley and for us! There is something within us that knows that Christian love is more than what we think or even what we do. The cognitive and behavioral aspects of love are important: we know what love is through rational analysis, and we affirm that love is best expressed through volitional actions—love acts. But understanding love only from these two perspectives takes the heart out of love and, in essence, the heart out of Wesleyan theology. That is, our affections (which can be defined in Wesley as habituated emotions) influence our ability to love. Thus Wesleyan theology is never stoic; it does not seek to suppress the emotional element of life. It affirms that God uses our emotional experiences just as much as our rationality and our liberty. If love is at the center of Wesley's theology, then we must recognize that love includes affect. And thus a Wesleyan practical theology encompasses the renewal of the *whole* person in the context of Christian community. This experiential emphasis not only adds to our theological methodology (the "Quadrilateral") but also makes pastoral ministry in a Wesleyan paradigm unique.

Third, practical theology should be contextual. It is not as concerned with definitions of truth as determining context-sensitive embodiments of the Christian gospel.[21] Wesley did not attempt to find a static message (i.e., propositional theology) that endures unchanged over time, remaining the same in every situation; nor did he attempt to only construct a purely contextual theology that finds its primary resources in very particular conditions of human experience.[22] Wesley was sensitive to the implications of theology for Christian life and specific contexts, and his sensitivity to particular situations helped shape his theology so as to make it practical,[23] without sacrificing his deference to the rich Christian orthodox tradition.

John Wesley's example of being a truly *practical theologian,* then, can provide pastors today with a model of integrated balance. Theology always informs what we do. But what we do is never extricated from our theology. Pastors in the tradition will reflect Wesley's theology through their ministry practices.[24] Many pastors have a good understanding of Wesleyan theology, but they struggle with integrating that theology with their pastoral practices.[25] For example, one study has shown that a sample of pastors who placed a strong emphasis on preaching the doctrine of holiness were unable to see the impact of that holiness on their own practice of ministry.[26] Given that holiness denominations are concerned today about a loss of theological identity, the recovery of that theological identity must certainly and ultimately find its way into the life of a congregation, perhaps most significantly in pastoral practices of our ministers. In other words, our pastoral practices should reflect our Wesleyan theology—such integration *is* our identity!

In order to examine this thesis more specifically, we have invited seasoned pastors and professionals to write chapters on how pastoral practices are informed by John Wesley's theology. We have attempted to cover a wide range of topics, although they can only be representative and certainly not all-inclusive of the various tasks of pastoral work. As you will see, the authors are all practitioners—not uninformed theoretically or theologically—but all intensely involved in the day-to-day life of ministry in their unique contexts. We have included senior pastors, associates, counselors, district and assistant superintendents, past missionaries, past college presidents, and a professor or two (with pastoral experience). Some have specializations that make them "experts" in their fields; some were simply willing to reflect more broadly on aspects of ministry. We are grateful to all of them for their important and we believe significant and lasting contributions.

Pastor Jeff Crosno offers key insights into how we are to follow Wesley into the pulpit, as ones ordained to "Word and Sacrament." Pastor Phil Hamner gives us the gift of a concise but deep sacramental theology that can be contextualized and applied to multiple ministry settings. Pastor Paul Willis integrates the primacy of worship into a scheme of spiritual formation—aspects of ministry too easily kept distinct. Rev. Jeren Rowell offers a model of pastoral care deeply rooted in a Wesleyan worldview. Dr. Glena Andrews and Dr. Michael Pitts offer key insights in how Wesleyan theology informs our care and counsel of others, as well as care for ourselves and our families. Dr. Ed Robinson, Dr. Stan Rodes, and Dr. Rondy Smith show that leading, discipling, and administrating the church should be deeply informed by a biblical view of servanthood and character-modeling, and suggest that such a Christlike disposition should be embraced by Wesley's followers as imperative for effective ministry. Dr. Nell Sweeden, Dr. Dana Hicks, and Rev. Joy Wisehart show how Wesleyan theology, underscored by love, expresses itself in hospitality—to "the least of these," to those with special needs, and to those God is wooing into relationship and the "divine dance." Love extends itself to others. This includes specific contexts, such as multicultural settings and the inner city, as Dr. Carol Rotz, Dr. Mario Zani, and Rev. Jon Middendorf show.

We (Dr. Mark Maddix and Dr. Diane Leclerc) are blessed to work in a context where pastoral ministry is at the forefront of our ministerial education: our very purpose is to produce pastors for the present and the future of the denomination(s). Each professor in the Department of Religion is ordained and has pastored in his or her career and seeks to instill a pastor's heart in each of our students. We are grateful for the wonderful collegiality we share with them and others in the School of Theology and Christian Ministry. Northwest Nazarene University is very much our home. We are particularly grateful to our students in our Senior Capstone course (2012), for trying out this book before publication and for their helpful suggestions.

We are thankful to Beacon Hill Press of Kansas City for choosing to publish this second volume in our Wesleyan Paradigm series (the first being *Spiritual Formation: A Wesleyan Paradigm*). It is our prayer that this book will be a true help to pastors in a variety of contexts, including those who are on the educational journey to such a high calling. It is our great privilege to serve in a denomination that continues to support, encourage, equip, ordain, sustain, and nurture those called by God to shepherd her sheep. And we are thankful for a theological tradition that embraces such an optimism of grace that it sees laity and ministers alike and declares "there is neither Jew nor Greek, slave nor free, male nor female, for you are all one in Christ Jesus" (Gal. 3:28). We all share a purpose and a vision; you, the reader, are all important as God builds the kingdom through you. May God bless your ministry, your obedience, and your sacrifice.

Discussion Questions

1. What are the primary roles of a pastoral ministry informed by Wesleyan theology?

2. Based on Wesley's pastoral criterion of being an overseer, learner, and person of dispositions, how do these relate to your role as a pastor?

3. As you reflect on your ministry practices, what are some examples of Wesleyan theology informing your ministry practice? Are there some areas that do not reflect a Wesleyan theology?

4. Given the criterion of practical theology being transformative, holistic, and contextual, how does your ministry practice reflect this criterion?

Recommended Reading

Heitzenrater, Richard. *Wesley and the People Called Methodists.* Nashville: Abingdon Press, 1995.

Langford, Thomas A. *Practical Divinity: Theology in the Wesleyan Tradition.* Nashville: Abingdon Press, 1984.

Maddox, Randy L. *Responsible Grace: John Wesley's Practical Theology.* Nashville: Abingdon Press, 1994.

Maddox, Randy L., ed. *Rethinking Wesley's Theology for Contemporary Methodism.* Nashville: Kingswood Books, 1998.

two

ORDAINED TO WORD
PREACHING IN THE WESLEYAN SPIRIT

～

Jeff Crosno

For pastors claiming to be theological descendants of John Wesley, attempting to outline a distinctively Wesleyan approach to preaching poses obvious problems if the man himself is to be our exemplar. If revisiting the quarry from which we were mined means that we are challenged to go where Wesley went to do what Wesley did, I suspect that most of our ordination boards will soon be without any waiting list of potential candidates. Simply reciting the well-known statistics will make the case that Wesley is likely to remain without rival or peer when we consider the vigor and sheer tenacity required by his preaching ministry. Given that he spent five decades riding perhaps twenty thousand miles on horseback each year, delivering an average of eight hundred sermons to crowds numbering up to twenty thousand, we can safely imagine that very few would now be willing to accept a ministry role that would correspond to a day in the life of the preacher John Wesley.[1] And fewer still would be the number of pastors who would gladly begin that day following the example of Wesley's ministry by preaching their first of at least two or three sermons promptly at 5 a.m.! Add to this Wesley's practice of preaching what often seem rather densely argued, largely *doctrinal* sermons without the benefit of manuscript or notes, and any remaining eagerness to find and follow the trail of the master quickly dissipates for most contemporary preachers. The spirit indeed may be willing, but judging by the ubiquity of the baristas and coffee mugs standing ready near many of our worship venues it is hard enough for many of us to even believe in God before noon on Sunday. The problem for Wesley's heirs may be that *we already know far too much about Wesley!*

What then is to be done by the preacher wishing to adopt a thoroughly *Wesleyan* way of preaching? As with many of our other attempts to engage in what may be called *adjectival* theology, the effort to define what is truly *Wesleyan* about our commitments in the pastoral ministry of preaching often turns out to be something of an ecclesiastical Rorschach test. In this quest to remain objectively faithful to Wesley in our principles and methodology, the very things we identify as authentically Wesleyan often mirror our own preferences and convictions to a degree that is uncomfortably predictable. So our desire to appropriate the elusive Mr. Wesley (whose positions on issues in question may be conveniently drawn from what historians call the "early," "middle," or "late" periods of his ministry) in support of our agenda for ministerial practice may well be deserving of some measure of "enhanced interrogation techniques." For just like politics, all interpretations are *local* and inevitably reflect the biases and experience of those rendering their verdicts. And with this caveat in mind, we should not be surprised to find that using adjectives like *Wesleyan* to qualify theological categories under discussion rarely lead to uncontested outcomes. So the question remains and deepens: what can now be done by preachers intending to demonstrate fidelity to Wesley's legacy?

After returning to the primary sources to once again read both what Wesley has to say about his own ministry as well as the published sermons securing his reputation for "practical divinity" within the Methodist revival, the place to begin may be found in his famous insistence on being regarded as *homo unius libri,* "a man of one book." The significance Wesley found in this designation may perhaps be inferred from the fact that the now famous quotation containing this phrase can be found in the opening preface to the initial volume of his *Sermons on Several Occasions.*

> I am a spirit come from God and returning to God; just hovering over the great gulf, till a few moments hence I am no more seen—I drop into an unchangeable eternity! I want to know one thing, the way to heaven—how to land safe on that happy shore. God himself has condescended to teach the way: for this very end he came from heaven. He hath written it down in a book. O give me that book! At any price, give me the Book of God! I have it. Here is knowledge enough for me. Let me be *homo unius libri.*[2]

Recognizing at the outset that the Wesley who speaks in this fashion is nonetheless a very erudite and well-read scholar entitled to wear the robe of an Oxford don, Wesley's lifelong passion as a lover of the biblical text is certainly present here. But neither is it hard to collect additional evidence of Wesley's thorough engagement with the Scriptures once we begin to look more closely at the commitments of his ministerial life. Randy Maddox has helpfully enumerated some of the ways in which this "man of one book" demonstrates that commitment to the primacy of the Scriptures in ways that also inform his practice as a preacher.

- Reading the Bible of his day (the King James Version), Wesley also values a range of other translations in English, German, and French.
- Wesley's fluency as an Oxford lecturer working with the Hebrew and Greek texts of the Bible apparently inspires him to develop abridged Greek and Hebrew grammars as part of the curriculum he prescribes at the Kingswood School providing

education *for the children of the coal miners to whom he regularly preached.*

- Wesley's reliance on the scholarly tools associated with the concerns of the newly emerging field of textual criticism becomes evident when the English translation he provides for his *Explanatory Notes upon the New Testament* varies from the King James Version in over twelve thousand instances![3]

Summarizing these as well as several other, similar indications regarding Wesley's obvious immersion in Scripture, Maddox reminds us that "John Wesley insisted that a good theologian must be a good *textuary* (student of biblical texts)."[4] But after reading Wesley's standard published sermons, it is also plain to see that this "one book" to which the preacher had devoted himself had clearly become the vital wellspring of his pulpit vocabulary, illustrations, and imagery.[5] In fact, when we take time to examine Wesley's recordkeeping regarding the texts appropriated in his preaching ministry, the breadth of his scriptural *preaching canon* becomes simply staggering. For if explicitly Wesleyan preaching means that we intend to follow Wesley's well-documented lead, we might begin to suspect that a good many preachers will be scrambling to log sermons in every book of the Bible *except* Esther, Song of Solomon, Obadiah, Nahum, Zephaniah, Philemon, and the Third Epistle of John![6] Should we therefore suggest that Wesleyan preaching is *methodical*?

Perhaps the better advice for us would be to consider this evidence of John Wesley's commitments as a "textuary" (interpreter) for what it implies *descriptively* rather than *prescriptively* regarding the ministry of preaching. In other words, the proper task assigned for preachers by our attention to Wesley is not that we seek in our own context to replicate with exacting precision what he did *but that we seek to become what he was.* Some, but certainly not all of those preachers who would today identify themselves as theological or ecclesiastical heirs of Wesley will be blessed with the kind of educational preparation and native gifts of intellect and temperament that he represents. But while only some of these preachers might be willing to suggest that their own academic experience and capacity is comparable to the original Oxford Methodist, any of Wesley's descendants may take advantage of opportunity to become the kind of passionate "textuary" that we are describing. In doing so, we will likely discover that the spirit of Wesley's example as *homo unius libri* proves to be quite suggestive for preachers in very helpful ways.

Having established the point that Wesley's engagement with Scripture was the work of an "amateur" (in the original French meaning of the phrase, which speaks of someone laboring for love of the task rather than the result of purely "professional" or commercial interests), we are not surprised when we learn that he completed his New Testament translation by working in sixteen-hour days while "convalescing" after he had suffered a near fatal illness in 1753.[7] What comes across in analyzing that unique translation project is that Wesley clearly remains an enthralled lover of the text, a man fully motivated by the engagement with Scripture as a means of grace. But again, while few contemporary preachers may possess the requisite skills to pursue this kind of textual work in their ministry, Wesley has shown us what it looks like to enter more deeply into that "Book of God" that so captured his attention. Therefore, it may also be wise for us to ask whether Wesley's pattern of reading Scripture *as a means of grace* continues to inform the exegetical process contributing to our ministry of preaching. What we have in mind here is whether or not the process of preparing to preach is more conducive to the minister's efforts to *explain* a passage than it is at enabling the preacher to *experience* the text. Unfortunately, many preachers continue to think that the job of the exegete is to *explore* the text while the job of the preacher is merely to *explain* the text.[8] But given the passion for the text that Wesley exudes within his work, presumably his concern for "practical divinity" begins first in the pastor's study.

Now allowing for the fact that Wesley preached effectively over the course of his lifetime out of a fairly well stocked "sermon barrel," we should show some measure of sympathy for contemporary pastors contending with the ongoing demand to develop something gripping and new to preach on a weekly basis.[9] But despite this pressure, is it not appropriate to suggest that a Wesleyan approach to preaching requires the preacher to remain a lover of the text rather than an interrogator now ready to *water-board* the passage to determine what secrets it might be withholding? It simply seems antithetical to the spirit of Wesley for us to expect pulpit intelligence to be supplied by preachers who prefer to torture truth out of their texts. Perhaps we should instead desire that Wesleyan preachers practice taking their sweet time to explore and experience what the text might freely wish to say when there is no threat or coercion within the relationship between preacher and passage. Speaking about these options for the preachers she is training, Anna Carter Florence recently described the tension we face in this way:

> Preachers who take on the role of explaining the text also take on the role of providing for their congregations; textually speaking, they may even be the sole provider. Every Sabbath, without fail, they have to come up with an answer that will feed a crowd for a week . . . They have to be good providers. They have to get that explanation, and by any means necessary. . . . [But] *if we preachers set ourselves up as the ones who explain the meaning of a text, then we slowly but surely kill our own relationship with the Word of God.*[10]

Or to put it another way, as we think about Wesley's characteristic approach in reading the Scriptures as the oracles of God, we notice that a critical difference still exists between preachers attempting to approach a text to determine what it *means* and those trying to be receptive to what that text may be *saying* to us. As Eugene Peterson notes, when pulpit exegesis is properly understood, it does not mean that we master a text but rather that we submit to the text as it has been given to us. And in this sense, we might say that a truly Wesleyan approach to the exegetical process of preparing a sermon can be recognized as an act of "sustained humility."[11]

While it may seem slightly odd in our rather exhibitionistic, celebrity-obsessed culture to speak seriously of *humility* while talking about preachers and their work, this may be precisely the point at which we should begin to consider the ultimate goal of Wesley's pulpit ministry. By now, several of the significant features of Wesley's public performance as a preacher have been documented. For example, it has now become traditional if not almost obligatory for historians to observe that Wesley's preaching gifts were certainly overshadowed by the homiletical flair of his contemporary, George Whitefield.[12] The conventional interpretation on this point usually goes on to affirm that the organizational genius demonstrated in Wesley's ability to create an effective infrastructure for discipleship (in the Methodist classes and bands) resulted in a conservation of the spiritual and numerical gains of the revival that went far beyond the initial impact of Whitefield's superior preaching. This emphasis upon structures that preserved and assisted growth in grace among those who clearly anticipated the possibility that they might be perfected in love is at the center of what Wesley meant with his famous aphorism that there is no holiness but "social holiness." But what has not always been clearly remembered about this distinctive feature of Wesley's preaching ministry is that Wesley himself tested the results of the Methodist revival when he spent two or three experimental years carefully monitoring the yield produced by "field-preaching" without a corresponding emphasis on setting up his societies. Finally calling off this experiment in 1748, he gravely explained his rationale in returning to the priorities of his earlier organizational work: "I was more convinced than ever that the preaching like an apostle, without joining together those that are awakened and training them up in the ways of God, is only begetting children for the murderer."[13]

In light of Wesley's discovery in this matter, for all the acclaim that we shower on effective preachers, a characteristically Wesleyan appraisal of pulpit ministry must recognize with real humility the significant *limitations* of preaching. Yet Wesley's modesty regarding the lasting impact of his preaching must also be balanced by mention of his insistence that the truth of his preaching on Christian perfection was confirmed in the transformed lives of his listeners.

> I do preach to as many as desire to hear, every night and morning. You ask; what would I do with them: I would make them virtuous and happy, easy in themselves and useful to others. Whither would I lead them? To heaven; to God the Judge, the lover of all, and to Jesus the Mediator of the new covenant. *What religion do I preach? The religion of love* [italics mine]; the law of kindness brought to light by the gospel. *What is this good for? To make all who receive it enjoy God and themselves: to make them like God; lovers of all* [italics mine].[14]

This consistent emphasis on "the religion of love" that Wesley came to expect as a result of his ministry helps explain why his famous resistance to the "sweetmeats" of so-called gospel preaching never descended into the all-too-familiar strictures of pulpit legalism.[15] As Mildred Bangs Wynkoop observed a generation ago, Wesley explained his essential pulpit strategy in replying to the question, "In what manner should we preach sanctification?": "Scarce at all to those who are not pressing forward; and to those who are, *always by way of promise; always drawing, rather than driving* [italics mine]."[16]

Given this Wesleyan confidence regarding the restorative effects of sanctifying grace on the "affections" and "tempers," to preach today as Wesley once preached might be to retain his insistent emphasis on making scriptural holiness apparent as a gracious privilege now available to every Christian. And by implication, the theological trajectory imagined within this kind of optimistic preaching seems to call for the preacher to *build an altar in every sermon*. Whether or not such an altar requires any sort of explicit response in the liturgy of a gathered congregation, the preacher has already determined that a mark of authentic Wesleyan preaching is that it anticipates "a Christianity of radical transformation."[17] As a result, we can expect that the form taken by this kind of preaching will differ significantly from other preaching forms that have lately become common within the Wesleyan-Holiness tradition. For at the risk of provoking at least a minor theological fistfight, the implications arising from this type of preaching for transformation signal something very important regarding our soteriological assumptions. By comparison, we may wish to ask if the now familiar Power-Point and fill-in-the-blank sermons suggest to our congregants that we are actually saved by *illumination*, by the disclosure of previously hidden *gnosis*, or knowledge.

> [But] Christians historically have claimed that the essential human problem is not lack of knowledge but a lack of will. It is not that we have momentarily misplaced the map of life and need to stop in at a spiritual convenience store for directions, but that we, as the classic prayer puts it, have "erred and strayed from your ways like lost sheep, and we have followed too much the devices and desires of our own hearts" . . . So we need not only knowledge, but also repentance and redemption.[18]

While there is much more that we could say about this key objective for preaching that embodies the stated convictions of Wesley, it may be wise to bring this chapter to a close by mentioning our hope for an obvious congruence between our distinctive theological witness and the *person* of the preacher. The kind of Wesleyan preaching we are envisioning is that which contributes meaningfully to the *confidence* of those who have been invited to partake of "the divine nature" (2 Pet. 1:4) through the sanctifying grace of the Holy Spirit. In short, we are asserting that *the preacher's own formation in holiness is a minimum prerequisite for entering the pulpit.* But this cannot be a recent innovation, given the conclusion drawn by Hughes Oliphant Old as he analyzes Wesley's sermon, "Christian Perfection."

> One wonders if a couple thousand coal miners standing out in the cold weather could possibly have been interested in all this. Evidently plenty of people in those crowds were. And after all, should we really be surprised? *When a man, who himself glows with holiness, opens up the way for others to follow, should we really be surprised when suddenly all other considerations fall away* [italics mine]?[19]

Discussion Questions

1. Despite the caution expressed by the author regarding our desire to engage in "adjectival" theologizing, what elements would you have initially identified as key contributions to a uniquely "Wesleyan" way of preaching?

2. What features of your present life would have to change for you to become the kind of "textuary" (student of scriptural texts) that we see in John Wesley's passionate commitment to reading Scripture as a means of grace?

3. In what ways would Wesley's preaching strategy to help his listeners grow in the sanctifying grace of a "religion of love" challenge or reaffirm what you believe to be important for contemporary "holiness preaching"?

4. Given that the life of the preacher may contribute to the confidence of listeners who are seeking to grow in the grace of holiness, to what degree do you share the author's conviction

that "the preacher's own formation in holiness is a minimum prerequisite for entering the pulpit"?

Recommended Reading

Collins, Kenneth J. *The Theology of John Wesley: Holy Love and the Shape of Grace.* Nashville: Abingdon Press, 2007.

Green, Joel B. *Reading Scripture as Wesleyans.* Nashville: Abingdon Press, 2010.

Maddox, Randy L. *Responsible Grace: John Wesley's Practical Theology.* Nashville: Abingdon Press, 1994.

Pasquarello, Michael. *John Wesley: A Preaching Life.* Nashville: Abingdon Press, 2010.

three

ORDAINED TO SACRAMENT
WESLEYAN THEOLOGY AS SACRAMENTAL PRACTICE

~

Phil Hamner

The challenge for every pastor in leading a congregation to raise up faithful disciples of Jesus Christ is to discover the regular and ordinary means by which the Holy Spirit engages, empowers, and strengthens the church and her members individually. The good news on this front is that pastor and congregation can find comfort and support in the long and storied tradition of the church. From her earliest days the church of Jesus Christ has known that in the regular practices of worship and discipleship God's Spirit is at work.

These regular practices, known as the means of grace, are essential to the life of Christianity in the Wesleyan tradition. When Wesleyan Christians gather in corporate worship, they engage in specific actions identified by the Spirit as the ordinary ways in which God speaks into the lives of his children. What are these regular ways? Scripture, prayer, and the sacraments find themselves as the primary means of grace. Scripture provides the fundamental ground to our worship and discipleship life. We are people of the book. We are guided by the book. We are strengthened and encouraged by the Word who gives the word. Prayer, too, serves the life of the Christian just as essentially as does breathing. Speaking to God and receiving a word from God is the breathing in and out of Christian existence.

What about the sacraments? What are they for the Wesleyan Christian? Why do we practice them? What purpose do they serve? For too many Wesleyan Christians the sacraments are a distant or occasional activity. They are practiced so infrequently that they carry no significant role or purpose in discipleship and worship in the life of the believing community. When they are practiced, they are activities done as if they were our doing, our idea, our clever and creative notions.[1]

Thankfully, this is not the case everywhere. Many churches are rediscovering the sacramental life. People are more regularly eating and drinking at the table of the Lord. Some of my pastoral colleagues have felt the Spirit's leading in celebrating the sacraments more frequently. Whatever the impetus for sacramental renewal, the Wesleyan tradition has a strong connection to baptism and Holy Communion as real means of grace.

The purpose of this essay is to make the case again for the place, meaning, and function of the sacraments in Wesleyan spirituality. First, we will put the sacraments within the Wesleyan tradition as a regular means of grace. Second, we will discuss baptism as the sacrament of initiation. Thus, we will argue for infant baptism as a biblical, historical, and pastoral practice for Wesleyan Christians. Third, we will identify the sacrament of Holy Communion as the regular means of sanctifying grace. Finally, we will offer some practical suggestions for sacramental renewal within Wesleyan churches.

What Is a Sacrament?

In the first place, Wesleyan churches receive their sacramental understandings through their spiritual father, John Wesley. For Wesley, an Anglican priest and leader of the Holiness Revival of the eighteenth century, a sacrament is "an outward sign of an inward grace, and a means whereby we receive the same."[2] This definition, of course, was Wesley's abridgment of the Anglican catechism on sacraments. But it points to the fact that Wesley understood the place and purpose of sacraments from the larger Anglican theological tradition. Beyond this Wesley believed baptism and the Lord's Supper to be "the appointed ways" or given by "divine appointment."

Sacramental life in the Wesleyan tradition always has its foundation in Christ himself. As Wesley argues, "Christ . . . alone has power to institute a proper sacrament, a sign, seal, pledge, and means of grace, perpetually obligatory on all Christians."[3] The "outward sign" then is a representation of Christ's institution, of Christ's doing. Water, bread, and wine are the symbols God uses to bring to mind (remembrance) the great work of Christ on the Cross. They are also the symbols of Christ's continuing presence and power in the community of faith.

Another important distinction to make about sacraments in the Wesleyan tradition is the use of the term "sacrament" itself. The term "sacrament" is preferred, following Wesley, over against the term "ordinance." The distinction is quite significant concerning the nature of grace. For Wesleyans sacraments represent God's initiative. Sacraments are "divine acts directed toward humanity as a way of ultimately sanctifying us."[4] This reflects the deep conviction that God's grace is always on the initiative to bring all people under the Lordship of Jesus Christ.

Those who favor the term "ordinance" favor a view of grace that is in contradiction with the Wesleyan understanding as such. Ordinances are "human acts directed from believers toward God as a way of giving testimony to the world."[5] This means the actions with water, bread, and wine are primarily human actions of devotion. This cannot fully or adequately represent Wesley's view, because the action begins with humanity.

The sacramental perspective reminds the church that salvation begins and ends with the triune God. When the church claims to be the beneficiary of God's saving acts in Jesus Christ, it is proclaiming this only by God's doing. So, when water, bread, and wine are used in the sacred acts of worship, they are a constant and continual reminder that we are gathered by God the Father; redeemed by God the Son;

and sanctified by God the Spirit. Yes, we are called to cooperate with God's grace, but only after he speaks first.

The Sacrament of Baptism

The first sacramental practice in the life of the church is baptism. It takes first place, because it is the sacrament of initiation. By bathing in the waters of baptism the Christian confirms his or her covenant with God. God has first spoken in Jesus Christ and continues to speak through the Holy Spirit. Baptism represents the introduction of a person's life into the life of God.

As such, baptism is only to be administered once. It signifies a birth into the believing community. Furthermore, baptism as the sign of God's action need not be repeated just because of the failure of the recipient. Water baptism brings to the community and to the individual the promise of what God has done and what God will do. Geoffrey Wainwright sets out Wesley's understanding of the benefits of the initiatory sacrament as, "It is a 'free gift' for 'washing away the guilt of original sin by the application of the merits of Christ's death' and 'the ordinary instrument of our justification.'"[6]

The question always arises whether baptism is necessary for salvation. Such a question belongs to an age that must categorize everything as necessary to achieve the desired result. The New Testament church would understand nothing of such questions. They would not comprehend arguments of the thief on the cross being promised paradise by Jesus as justification for baptism being optional. What is most compelling to the conversation about baptism's necessity is captured by Wesley's conviction that baptism was the "sign, seal, pledge and means of grace, perpetually obligatory on all Christians."[7]

The proper understanding of the relationship between the outward sign of water baptism with the inward sign of new birth or conversion is that which is demonstrated by the early church. On that point Wesley captures the heartbeat of New Testament conviction. Namely, baptism is commanded of the Lord as the primary means through which God's grace is active in the life of the church. While neither the New Testament nor Wesley argues that baptism magically creates new birth, neither does either dismiss baptism as unnecessary or optional for the community and the individual.

Baptism is represented in the New Testament as essential to the discipleship of the individual and the worship life of the community. With this in mind some have reduced the response to Peter's sermon on the Day of Pentecost as a sort of formula for conversion. Peter calls for a strong and decisive response to his message: repentance and baptism, which will then lead to the reception of forgiveness and the Holy Spirit. Yet, as William Willimon is quick to point out,

> This pattern of conversion appears nowhere else in Acts. Elsewhere when Luke recounts the conversion of a crowd he merely says that many believed (4:4; 5:14) or that they turned to the Lord (9:35). Here is no order-of-salvation, but rather a conclusion of Peter's speech. In his speech Peter has asserted the guilt of the Jerusalemites for the death of Jesus (2:22-23, 36). When they ask what they must do, the context makes clear that something must be done about their guilt.[8]

One other point is pertinent at this juncture related to the order of actions with respect to baptism. It is generally considered that baptism comes after repentance and faith as the normal or appropriate means of conversion. That is, the Holy Spirit must make us alive before we can partake of the sacrament. Again, Willimon makes the point quite clear.

> Luke knows no clear-cut pattern of how and when the Spirit is given. Acts 10:44-48 shows Cornelius and his family receiving the Spirit *before* they were baptized. But in Acts 19:5-6 the Spirit comes on the disciples of John the Baptist when Paul lays his hands on them after their baptism. Surely this diversity within

Luke-Acts is testimony to the diversity and freedom of the experience of the Spirit within the church of Luke's day.[9]

One additional viewpoint is necessary here to help the Wesleyan Christian understand the power and importance of their theological heritage. This other viewpoint fills in the rich significance of the very notion of baptism as the sacrament of initiation. Rob Staples in his significant and groundbreaking work on the sacraments for the Church of the Nazarene argues convincingly for the fivefold dimension of baptism as initiation. This fivefold dimension is as follows:

(1) It is the mark of our inclusion in the new covenant that Christ established. (2) It is the symbol of our identification with the death of Christ. (3) It is the symbol of our participation in the resurrected life of Christ. (4) It is the symbol of our reception of the Holy Spirit, which is the Spirit of Christ. (5) It is the action through which we are made part of Christ's Body, the Church.[10]

With the wealth of imagery that one finds in the Wesleyan tradition concerning baptism, one would do well to reengage the tradition for the sake of sacramental renewal. This kind of renewal can breathe life into the worshiping community and give strength to the journey of discipleship for the individual in God's kingdom. If one takes seriously the power of enacting the gospel in the sacrament, then there is one other piece of the baptismal life of the church that must be reconsidered and embraced fully again within Wesleyan circles.

The Place and Purpose for Infant Baptism

Infant baptism has been the point of great tension in nearly all the churches of the Wesleyan-Holiness tradition. The tension grows out of competing convictions about the nature of the church. Yet, the longer Wesleyan tradition has always embraced the practice as a sign and seal of the promise of the covenant God has made through Jesus Christ. Infant baptism carries doctrinal support in many of the denominational guidebooks for faith and practice. So, why has the clearly baptistic practice of infant dedication taken over the place of ritual in these various bodies? In other words, why have clearly non-Wesleyan practices been given preference in the liturgical practices of most Wesleyan churches?

The simple answer to this question is that we have ignored our own theological heritage in favor of a more psychologically satisfying answer. In a culture where we believe that only fully adult individuals can make rational and appropriate decisions after they have been given all the facts, the very idea of initiation into the community of faith as one enters the world seems like a reach.

Faith is not about a cafeteria-style selection process where the participant is given a vast array of information that he or she must sift through to make a decision. Rather, biblical faith has to do with being born into the world graced by the mercy of a loving God. Believing parents, then, as faithful representatives of the believing community bring their children for initiation into the body, but this is not an act of their own doing. This is a responsive act of parents to the gracious mercy of God in Jesus Christ. Parents then do not act primarily as the spiritual leaders of their own household—though they are—but rather as members of the household of God.

So, what does the Wesleyan heritage give us concerning the practice of infant baptism? For the full answer to this we must return again to John Wesley. First, Wesley confirms and puts forward the teaching of the larger Anglican tradition that infants are also subjects of baptism, because "'in Adam all die;' that 'by one man's disobedience all were made sinners . . . This plainly includes infants; for they too die; therefore they have sinned.'"[11] This understanding of universal sinfulness maintains the integrity of our theology to our evangelical heritage as well.

Second, the Wesleyan heritage reminds us that infants are proper subjects for baptism, because they, too, are heirs of the covenant God made with Abraham. On this point Wesley writes,

The infants of believers, the true children of faithful Abraham, always were under the gospel covenant. They were included in it, they had a right to it and to the seal of it; as an infant heir has a right to his estate, though he cannot yet have actual possession . . . In this covenant children were also obliged to what they knew not, to the same faith and obedience with Abraham. And so they are still; as they are still equally entitled to all the benefits and promises of it.[12]

Third, Wesley believed that since infants were proper subjects of a covenant with God, they are also capable of coming to God. On the authority of Matt. 19:13-14 and Luke 18:15 Wesley was convinced infants were then capable of admission into the church by means of baptism. On this point he writes, "If infants ought to come to Christ, if they are capable of admission into the Church of God, and consequently of solemn sacramental dedication to him, then they are proper subjects of baptism. But infants are capable of coming to Christ, of admission into the Church, and solemn dedication to God."[13]

Fourth, the Wesleyan tradition is committed to the doctrine and practice of infant baptism, because the practice was plainly practiced by the apostles.[14] John Wesley was under no illusion that the New Testament does not explicitly identify infants as recipients of baptism. He does, however, assert that the practice was implicit in the New Testament church. On this point he notes, "That the Jews admitted proselytes by baptism as well as by circumcision, even whole families together, parents and children, we have the unanimous testimony of their most ancient, learned, and authentic writers."[15] Not only has circumcision been superseded by the new covenant symbol of baptism, but the proselyte baptisms would also be superseded by baptism into Jesus Christ.

Finally, Wesley reaches deep within the Christian tradition to affirm that Christians in all places and all ages have made infant baptism their general practice.[16] This appeal to the larger Christian church reminds Wesleyan Christians that the commitments of Wesley are not strange, abnormal, or caricatured images of the Christian faith. They stand fully with the faith of Christians in all ages.

The Sacrament of Holy Communion

If baptism is the sacrament of initiation, then for the Wesleyan tradition Holy Communion is the sacrament of sanctification. Unlike baptism, which is to be administered only once in the life of a person, Holy Communion is to be practiced often and regularly. When speaking of Holy Communion as the sacrament of sanctification, the aspect being spoken of is the progress work of sanctification. This means that the very work of the Holy Spirit enables growth in grace at all points along the Christian journey. As Rob Staples writes, "The Eucharist may be understood as that means of grace, instituted by Jesus Christ, to which we are invited for repentance, for self-examination, for renewal, for spiritual sustenance, for thanksgiving, for fellowship, for anticipation of the heavenly kingdom, and for celebration in our pilgrimage toward perfection in the image of Christ."[17]

So then, Holy Communion accompanies the church and the individual along the journey toward eternal life. The actions surrounding the bread and wine represent the various ways in which grace is at work and present in our lives. From the earliest days of the Wesleyan revival John Wesley advocated that those with "some degree of repentance and faith should partake of the Lord's Supper."[18] Since Jesus commanded the regular and frequent practice of Holy Communion, this meant that persons at all stages of Christian development would encounter the shaping practice of eating bread and drinking the cup. In fact, Wesley defended an open table so that people could respond to the grace of God in their lives. In this way he writes, "The Lord's Supper was ordained by God to be a means of conveying to men either preventing or justifying, or sanctifying grace, according to their several necessities."[19]

Much has been made that persons must deeply examine themselves before they are allowed to come to the table of the Lord. And, indeed, Holy Communion was never intended to be a trivial or frivolous encounter. The table of the Lord was also not meant to be a place where only those who have "cleaned up their act" are allowed to partake. Since Christ's meal was intended for the sanctification of his bride, the ongoing and regular eating and drinking will cause the strengthening of the individual and the holiness of the church. Similarly, Wesley writes, "The persons for whom it [Holy Communion] was ordained are all those who know and feel that they want the grace of God, either to restrain them from sin, or to show their sins forgiven, or to renew their souls in the image of God."[20]

The interaction of the communicant with the elements of bread and wine, or more importantly with the presence of Christ in the meal, was also intended to produce a people zealous for good works in the world. In the very name of the meal, Holy *Communion*, we discover the importance of fellowship, of sharing, of participation. This participation is with Christ and with other believers in cooperation for the redemption of the world. The frequency and consistency, then, of the meal as worship and discipleship gives us the place of our sustenance. The meal "denotes spiritual nutrition and formation as God's people, fed and prepared to serve God at every opportunity."[21] Christ's ongoing presence in the regular actions of the church's life together necessitates active response by the people of God. This we do know: "Christ is actively present so that we may be more actively present in the mission of the church to the world."[22]

Finally, the practice of Holy Communion was intended to sustain a consistency and fidelity from its earliest days of practice. This was not an institutional action in order to gain control over the worship life of the individual churches. Rather, consistency and fidelity to Christ's intention for the meal has meant a consistency and fidelity with apostolic teaching. This was Wesley's desire for the meal for his Methodist societies and churches in America.

So, what does fidelity to early church practice mean? It first means a remembering of the words and actions of Christ (*anamnesis*). We are to call to mind the purpose of the meal by the very words of Jesus Christ himself. Second, we are to remember this meal is a thanksgiving (*Eucharist*). Jesus gave thanks for the bread and wine, and we are to offer our prayer at the meal as thanksgiving. Third, we are to celebrate the unity of the body of Christ (*koinonia*) as it gathers together in eating and drinking. Finally, we are to invoke the presence and power of the Holy Spirit (*epiclesis*) in order for Christ to be present in the bread and wine and in the believing community. This has been an important missing element in much of the Wesleyan tradition. Without the *epiclesis* we have failed to "call upon the Holy Spirit to make the bread and wine 'to be for us the body and blood of Christ' so that we, the communicants, in turn may be 'the body of Christ for the world.'"[23]

Suggestions for Practice and Renewal of Sacramental Life

Sacramental life is essential for the promotion and growth of Christian life from the Wesleyan perspective. Thus far in this essay we have attempted to make the case for the strong and vibrant biblical, theological, and practical implications for renewal of sacramental action within the body of churches in the Wesleyan tradition. It seems appropriate now to make several suggestions for future practice and renewal in our churches. This comes at a time when Wesleyan churches for many reasons have lost their liturgical and theological way.

First, the current interest and rediscovery of Holy Communion is to be commended and encouraged. Many churches are reporting eucharistic meals more frequently in the life of the church. Over the past two decades Wesleyan-Holiness churches are realizing that Holy Communion is the normal response to the proclamation of the preached Word. We should remind ourselves, however, the sacramental practice is not a novelty, a neat thing, a clever idea that just needs some new clothing to dress itself up. With the increase in eucharistic frequency a set of strange and inappropriate practices have begun to develop. Individualistic family drop-in Communions, and come and go Communion times, for example, defy the very corporate nature of the meal. Koinonia is damaged. The place of the Eucharist as the response to the preached Word is fractured.

Other practices, such as extensive multimedia presentations and musical packages can too easily overtake the words and actions of breaking bread and serving the cup. The rediscovery of sacramental practice is a really good outcome for the church, but the rediscovery should be accomplished within the context of Wesleyan faith and practice. That means a reintroduction of the words of sacramental life. The eucharistic prayer should begin with the comforting and challenging words of invitation.

> You that do truly and earnestly repent of your sins, and are in love and charity with your neighbors, and intend to lead a new life, following the commandments of God, and walking from henceforth in his holy ways: Draw near with faith, and take this Holy Sacrament to your comfort, and make your humble confession to almighty God.[24]

We should celebrate and embrace our rich and deep heritage for what it is. It is an aid and tool to raise up deeply committed Christians in the Wesleyan tradition. The careful and consistent leadership of pastors in the work of the pulpit and the table will result in people who see the world through the eyes of Christ. Wesleyan emphases in sacred actions of the table will give us the language of grace, mercy, and holiness in our daily living and ministry in the world.

Second, sacramental renewal in the Wesleyan tradition must include a renewed emphasis on discipleship in the Wesleyan mode. The acts of worship that make up sacramental practice will not by themselves cause the deep renewal we desire in our churches. The Wesleyan connection of Bible study and accountability are necessary to make sense of kingdom actions of water, bread, and wine. It will be the community in worship *and* the community in discipleship that brings the sense of holiness of heart and life alive in the church.

Finally, sacramental renewal in the Wesleyan tradition will need a redirection of our pastoral emphases away from "what works" toward "what deepens." Too many of us in the pastoral office feel pressure, both externally and internally, to produce statistical growth that does not always represent real growth in grace. Those actions that deepen the life of the individual and the life of the worshiping community will not necessarily be those actions that bring the quick results we are so encouraged to embrace. Genuinely deepening actions in worship and discipleship take days and weeks and years to produce deep Christians in the Wesleyan tradition. We must be patient, so that the very love of God can do its great work in us.

Discussion Questions

1. Why do Wesleyans insist on using the term "sacraments" rather than "ordinances"?

2. If baptism is the sacrament of initiation, what are persons being initiated into when they participate?

3. Why is infant baptism embraced by the Wesleyan tradition as the ordinary means of initiation and discipleship?

4. How does Holy Communion signify the nature of grace from the Wesleyan perspective?

5. Why is it essential to maintain fidelity in the actions and practices of Holy Communion?

Recommended Reading

Abraham, William J., and James E. Kirby. *The Oxford Handbook of Methodist Studies*. New York: Oxford University Press, 2009.

Borgen, Ole. *John Wesley on the Sacraments: A Definitive Study of John Wesley's Theology of Worship*. Grand Rapids: Francis Asbury Press, 1972.

Powell, Samuel M. *A Teacher's Guide to Understanding the Sacraments*. Kansas City: Beacon Hill Press of Kansas City, 2011.

Staples, Rob L. *Outward Sign and Inward Grace: The Place of Sacraments in Wesleyan Spirituality*. Kansas City: Beacon Hill Press of Kansas City, 1991.

Stookey, Laurence Hull. *Eucharist: Christ's Feast with the Church*. Nashville: Abingdon Press, 1993.

Wainwright, Geoffrey. *Eucharist and Eschatology*. London: Epworth Press, 2003.

four
RESPONSIVE TO GOD
WESLEYAN WORSHIP AS A MEANS OF SPIRITUALLY FORMING GRACE

~~~

Paul Willis

*As every seed produces fruit of a like nature, so the word of God must
daily produce in us new spiritual fruits. If we are to become new creatures
by faith, we must live in accordance with the new birth. In a word,
Adam must die, and Christ must live, in us. It is not enough to know
God's word; one must also practice it in a living, active manner.*
—Johann Arndt[1]

One of the beautiful aspects of the pastoral vocation is its practical,
down-to-earth nature. It is the nitty-gritty of pastoral ministry that is
most challenging and fulfilling. For Wesley, spiritual formation occurs
in the raw experiences of worshiping communities. Central to the heart
of pastors is the spiritual formation of the people God has placed under
their care. A key orienting concern for pastors is the spiritual formation
of the body of Christ. Pastors should focus on creating environments in
which spiritual formation can occur. This chapter reflects on distinct-
ly Wesleyan ways for pastors to promote spiritual formation in their
congregations, particularly through worship. Wesleyan theology deeply informs the practices of the pastoral office. The Wesleyan-Holiness
tradition offers rich soil in which Christian orthodoxy and orthopraxis
can flourish. It is the author's hope that these ideas will help clergy and
lay leaders maximize spiritual formation in their churches. Essentially,

the task of church leadership is the active modeling of holiness of heart and life. This is done through a lived-out faith and by creating environments in which moments and process of spiritual formation can occur.

How are churches and their pastors cultivating environments where Christian identity and vocation are formed? Is our leadership as pastors encouraging response to God's prevenient, justifying, and sanctifying grace? Upon these decisions, do we as pastors provide structures and environments in which those new in faith can grow and develop in Christian maturity? The Wesleyan-Holiness tradition offers an abundance of practices and disciplines pastors can utilize to promote spiritual formation in their congregations. Worship is certainly one of the most important.

Moments and Process

The Christian life is punctuated by moments in which individuals experience crises of faith; it is also characterized by a journey of faith in which growth in holiness occurs over a lifetime. By grace through faith we are justified, regenerated, and adopted into the family of God. As Christ followers who desire Christian maturity and entire sanctification, we enter into the process of being conformed to the image of Christ for the sake of others.[2] There are crisis moments in the faith life, times of recognition, response, and repentance; individual moments where by the grace of God we are freed from sin and brought into renewed relationship with God. We turn from that which is dishonoring to God, the sinful life, toward a reorienting concern of love for God, love for others, and self-denied service to both. Along with and often subsequent to, distinct crisis moments in the faith walk, we enter into the journey of Christian life, a process of maturity and sanctification. Among other roles, it is the responsibility of the pastor to create environments in worship experiences in which the Spirit works, where the moments and process of Christian faith formation occur and the process of maturity is nurtured.

Corporate Worship

The gathering of the church community for corporate worship creates a core liturgical framework out of which spiritual formation occurs. John Wesley valued corporate worship as a *means of grace* and an essential source of spiritual sustenance. For Wesley, it provided spiritual nurture that parishioners should abandon at their grave loss.[3] The pastor leads corporate worship, and in doing so, creates an environment where the body of Christ can engage in the formative liturgies of the church, including prayer, worship in song, engaging in the rhythms of the church year, and partaking in the sacramental life. "The *Sunday Service*, then, presents Wesley's mature pattern for weekly liturgical worship."[4] We gather together for mutual encouragement, accountability, fellowship, hearing God's Word, and to be reminded of the social dynamic of a life of holiness. We also remember that the Christian community exists because God calls it into being for the advancement and embodiment of Christ's ministry. Therefore, corporate worship is a response to divine initiative.

The Centrality of Prayer to Corporate Worship

Prayer led by the pastor of the faith community is central to corporate worship. Many understand prayer to be a communication between the individual and God, but there is deep value in pastor-led prayer within corporate worship. Thomas C. Oden articulates the value of prayer by the pastor in corporate worship. "Centuries of experience show that the laity best pray under the guidance of the apostolic tradition mediated by a prepared and informed ministry."[5] It is the pastor who "representatively intercede[s] on behalf of the faithful community before God in prayer as a timely, public, verbal, hearable act."[6] In corporate worship, the pastor gives voice and articulation to the prayers of the people before God. The pastor facilitates spiritual formation by acting as a "representative liturgist leading the community in prayer, and in doing so enables and facilitates their own praying."[7] The pastor offers prayers fitting to the community's needs, contrition, struggles, praises, and progress. The pastor gives "language, form, symbol, and expression to otherwise unspoken human experiences, by offering them symbolic interpretation in a community of prayer," in doing so facilitates spiritual formation.[8]

The Spiritually Formative Role of Preaching in Corporate Worship

For John Wesley, pastoral preaching was "focused on the worship setting of the society, providing encouragement and guidance for their growth in saving relationship to God."[9] Pastoral preaching invites people into relationship with God, convinces them of the necessity of Christian life, and nurtures their spiritual formation. Well-written and engagingly delivered sermons break down strongholds and nudge people into Spirit-empowered moments of Christian transformation. They then continue to guide and inspire people along the journey of Christian holiness. The sermon is a "means of grace in worship, communicating Christ, assuring us of God's pardoning love, while simultaneously revealing our remaining need, and leading our further growth in Christ-likeness."[10] When pastors preach, they are doing much more than disseminating scriptural information; they are calling people into participatory relationship and experience of God. Scriptural preaching draws from people a response to God, entering them into the story of God and God's self-revelation to creation. Pastors proclaim the good news that Jesus Christ is Lord—the public proclamation of Christian truth, spoken and contextualized to the present community of faith and to all who have ears to hear. "Preaching is a re-appropriation of the written word for the witnesses to the revealed word."[11] Preaching in corporate worship is a beautiful proclamation of the good news, calling people to Christ, offering a word of conviction, comfort, encouragement, and inspiration to Christian spiritual formation and discipleship. Preaching is bimodal, offering teaching and exposition of Scripture, while simultaneously fashioning a moral sensitivity in its hearers that increases awareness and elicits changed behavior.[12] Preaching is that beautiful, artistic, challenging, engaging, and spiritual discipline that ever remains central to corporate worship. Preaching calls people to repentance and response to God's prevenient and saving grace. It is a core Wesleyan distinctive; so pastors, preach!

A Renewed Voice: A Fresh Expression

The ancient practice of singing and lifting voices to God in worship is a powerfully formative spiritual practice. While many pastors do not serve as the worship/music leader of their congregations, they do and should oversee this facet of corporate worship. Whether it is creating consistency between song selection and sermon content, assisting with the creation of a reflective environment, or simply modeling worship in song to the congregation, the pastor has a pivotal role. Charles Wesley, the brother of John Wesley, introduced hymn singing to corporate worship. The practice was impressed on Wesley by a group of Moravians who were finding comfort in their hymn singing during their voyage to Georgia. "Upon arrival he published a *Collection of Psalms and Hymns* for his own congregation's worship."[13] Hymns became an integral part of Methodist corporate worship. Wesley understood worship in song to be a spiritually formative practice, empowering and shaping holy living. Music is emotive and universal; it literally can reflect the rhythms of the church universal. Singing provides a means to speak words of faith and Scripture as a unified body, praising God as one universal church. Pastors should embrace this aspect of corporate worship in all of its diversity, beauty, and expression. Encourage worship in song, do not be afraid to explore and traverse new ground, dive into older or more traditional hymns, mine their rich meaning, and give them fresh expression. Do not get caught in the old versus new debate. Sometimes a song can express what words alone cannot; a song's age is irrelevant!

One might think of worship music as Scripture, prayer, affirmation, and confession set to music.

Finding the Rhythms of the Church in Corporate Worship

There is significant value in the pastor of a faith community who engages the congregation in the rhythmic liturgies and calendar of the church year. It is like breathing. A healthy organism breathes; there is a rhythm to the expansion and contraction that brings in fresh oxygen and perpetuates life. The church calendar and associated liturgy have a similar rhythm, an expansion and contraction—breathing. Creation itself is full of order, systems, and rhythms: DNA, tides, lunar cycles, seasons, human birth and death. God seems to appreciate order, so should the church as the continued ministry of Jesus Christ.

Introducing the congregation to the larger story of the church connects them with the church universal; it enters them into the rhythms of the church calendar. The universal, overarching nature of the church calendar diverts attention from an individual's ability to produce or perform and refocuses it on worshiping corporately in the body of Christ. In doing so, we celebrate God's gift of salvation to humanity and enter into unfolding the whole mystery of Christ. "Congregational life is shaped around the ways it remembers certain events. The first has been the overwhelming adoption of the liturgical calendar in worship . . . liturgical seasons provide a structure for the continuing rehearsal of the primary stories of Christian community . . . it draws people away from producing church and enters them into the story of Christ."[14]

Naturally extending from a congregation whose corporate worship includes the church calendar is a pastor who is unafraid to engage the lectionary and formal liturgies. While we do not use liturgy for liturgy's sake, or for the perpetuation of tradition to that end alone, liturgy can be effectively used to point people to Christ and bring congregations into the rhythms of the larger church. Such a practice in corporate worship shifts the individual's focus onto the story of God and the community of faith. Thus, liturgies build unity, purpose, and identity as a community, not just as an individual. These practices connect the congregants of smaller and often disconnected NewStart churches with the larger story of Christianity and the church catholic. The liturgical calendar, lectionary, formal prayers, and even colors of the church seasons used in corporate worship connect congregations with the ancient traditions of the Christian faith. This develops an environment of spiritual formation, a type of surrogate heritage and sense of belonging. It develops a rootedness that focuses on who we are and where we come from, not on one's ability to produce. It creates a family whose growth and worship flow out of and within the rhythms of the church as a whole. When liturgies are fresh, creative, and feed the hungers of the human heart for Christ, they become intensely spiritually formative events. It should be noted that Wesley's agenda in reducing the number of "holy days" recognized in corporate worship was for increased simplicity, a "structuring of the church year around seasons tied directly to Christ—Advent, Easter, and Ascension/Pentecost."[15] Pastors should affirm the practice of remembering the story of the triune God through the rhythms of the church year. The contemporary church becomes connected to the ancient church by finding fresh ways of implementing these stories and by creating experiences for believers in which they can participate.

Spiritual Formation in the Community Outside of Traditional Worship

As we have seen, spiritual formation occurs during times of corporate worship and the Sunday service. However, John Wesley encouraged church leadership and pastors to nurture spiritual formation and Christian maturity seven days a week, not just on Sunday. This section focuses on spiritual formation in the faith community during the majority of its life outside of corporate worship.

A Renewed Life: Watch Night Services

Watch night services are periodic gatherings of the church that provide time for deeper contemplation on the Christian journey. They "provide a time of reflection—both to awaken us to remaining sin and to convince us of God's support in our renewed obedient response."[16] In our fast-paced culture, pastors need to nurture times of solitude, helping people find the quiet in their lives. We need regular times of self-examination, self-analysis, times where we seek God's revelation regarding our attitudes, heart condition, actions, and motivations. We need regular moments of confession and repentance. It is a powerful sign that spiritual formation is occurring in the church when conviction of sin becomes a deep-felt reality, when confession and repentance are practiced, and when people manifest radical humility and dependence on God. When this happens, people begin to pray for their towns, their people, and their world. It is then that *shalom begins to burst forth!* It only seems wise that pastors should integrate a service or time of gathering like this into the life of their local church.

Formation Through Fellowship: The Open Table

The term "open table" might be a more contemporary name for what John Wesley called love feasts. These are times when the church gathers for a meal and fellowship; it is a reflection and continuation of the early Christian *agape* meal. Where Wesley might have implemented stricter attendance requirements, the open table in a contemporary church could be freely attended by anyone interested in Christian fellowship or learning more about the church. It could consist of testimonies, praises, food, and fellowship, with the goal of nurturing relationships within the church body and the surrounding community. The meal was to represent the *power of one*—one community, one faith, one mission—and to "nourish us with social grace."[17]

The open table is a joyful celebration. Christ entered this world bringing good news of great joy, and he left the world bequeathing his joy to the disciples. John 15:11 says, "These things I have spoken to you that my joy may be in you, and that your joy may be full" (ESV). André Trocmé in *Jésus-Christ et la revolution non-violente* goes to great lengths to teach us of the importance of fellowship and joy, that Jesus began his public ministry by proclaiming the year of Jubilee.[18] Augustine wrote, "The Christian should be an alleluia from head to foot!" Being in Christian fellowship is celebratory because of our hope that is Christ Jesus. "To be conformed to the image of Christ for others not only calls us to the fullness of life in the body of Christ; it also thrusts us into the world as agents of God's healing, joyful, and transformative grace."[19] John Wesley taught that there is no holiness without social holiness. It is a joyful event to fellowship with Christians and to extend that fellowship to the world. As we live out our missional calling, we extend that joy and hope to others. We invite them freely into fellowship with ourselves and with those in our faith community—Christ freely invites all to fellowship with him; this is the theological impetus for the open table. This discipline centers on relationship development and the ancient practice of *table fellowship* and eating together. Although the pastor may not integrate the diversity of rules in traditional table fellowship, he or she should capture the idea of building relationships with the unchurched, sharing stories and meals together, and joyfully escorting those outside the faith into the community of believers. This liturgy of table fellowship requires parishioners to serve and be served, to host and be hosted, and to reach out to their neighbor and share time together. Table fellowships are not Bible studies or places of discipleship/accountability per se, but recognition that all humanity wants to be loved, accepted, and made to feel valuable. The purpose of the open table is to encourage relationship development that organically flows into the corporate worship services and discipleship groups. It is in the small groups where spiritual formation and the missional ecclesiology of the church can be lived out. John Wesley said, "God has given us to each other to strengthen each other's hands." In these ways, the pastor can form Christian liturgies that encourage healthy spiritual formation within the local church community.

Pastors have a wonderful opportunity to provide means of grace for the transformation of their people in public spaces. Worship and communal experiences are just as important as the more private means of grace, especially as we continue to battle an individualistic version of the Christian faith. But it is our responsibility to lead these well, so that our people begin to understand them as fulfilling the true purpose of spiritual growth and change.

Discussion Questions

1. Discuss what the author means by spiritual formation occurring in "moments and process." Describe your journey of Christian salvation and sanctification thus far.

2. What practices does the author suggest are central to spiritual formation in corporate worship? As a pastor or lay leader, how are you creating environments in which spiritual formation can occur?

3. What is meant by *rhythms* of the church and how might they be instrumental in helping church leadership facilitate spiritual formation in the faith community? How can liturgies be expressed in fresh, creative, and experiential ways?

4. For John Wesley the sacramental life of the church was essential. Are there ways your local church can increase or rejuvenate the practice of sacramental liturgies? How often is Communion offered in your services? Why?

5. Spiritual formation should happen during corporate worship, and according to John Wesley, every day of the week. Besides

midweek services or Bible studies, how is your leadership fostering Christian maturity among members of the congregation? What role might watch night services play?

6. What does the author mean by "formation through fellowship" and the "open table"?

Recommended Reading

Guder, Darrell L. *Missional Church: A Vision for the Sending of the Church in North America.* Grand Rapids: Eerdmans, 1998.

Hirsch, Alan. *The Forgotten Ways: Reactivating the Missional Church.* Grand Rapids: Brazos Press, 2006.

Leclerc, Diane, and Mark A. Maddix. *Spiritual Formation: A Wesleyan Paradigm.* Kansas City: Beacon Hill Press of Kansas City, 2011.

Maddox, Randy L. *Responsible Grace: John Wesley's Practical Theology.* Nashville: Abingdon, 1994.

Matthaei, Sondra Higgins. *Making Disciples: Faith Formation in the Wesleyan Tradition.* Nashville: Abingdon Press, 2000.

Mulholland, M. Robert, Jr. *Invitation to a Journey: A Road Map for Spiritual Formation.* Downers Grove, IL: InterVarsity, 1993.

Oden, Thomas S. *Pastoral Theology: Essentials in Ministry.* New York: HarperCollins, 1983.

Roxburgh, Alan J., and M. Scott Boren. *Introducing the Missional Church: What It Is, Why It Matters, How to Become One.* Grand Rapids: Baker Publishing Group, 2009.

Webber, Robert E. *Ancient-Future Time: Forming Spirituality Through the Christian Year.* Grand Rapids: Baker Publishing Group, 2004.

five
REPRESENTING GOD
PASTORAL CARE AS A WESLEYAN ESSENTIAL

~~⌒~~

Jeren Rowell

I am a pastor. Writing that sentence brightens my day. Hearing some-one address me or refer to me as *Pastor* is a heartwarming experience. It may not be quite to the level of hearing some particular little ones call me *Papa*, but it's close. The reasons for this are not sentimental. My esteem for the idea of pastor is neither about nostalgia nor privilege. It is more about holy reverence for a calling to serve God's people in a particular way that I soon learned had no genesis in my ability apart from God. It is a profound grace to be called to the office of pastor in the church; a grace for which I remain thankful even now, as a district superintendent, as my pastoral calling is fulfilled among a connection of congregations and no longer in one parish.

One cannot think rightly about *pastoral care* unless and until one begins to think rightly about *pastor*. The theology and practice of pastor today may be on the verge of recovering from a long stretch of sub-servience to popular conceptions of organizational leadership (at least in North American culture, i.e., pastor as CEO). These conceptions, while useful in many ways, are on their own found wanting in terms of their ability to bear the weight of what pastoral care calls us to be and to do. This is because pastoral care is not essentially a set of skills or practices that anyone can adapt from a business model and learn to apply in the context of congregation and community. Pastoral care is theologically rooted in the shared life of our triune God. The relationship of holy love shared by Father, Son, and Spirit is the basis from which all other loves spring, including the love that calls forth pastors out of the community of faith and then back into the community of faith as servants. Therefore, the love that enables authentic pastoral care is more than warm feelings for people or for certain tasks. Rather, pastoral love is a commitment (perhaps we could say *covenant*) to serve people in ways that promote the realization of "Thy kingdom come." This kind of servant leader, called by God and enabled by the Spirit, provides not only for the administration of word and sacrament but also for the kind of shepherding ministry modeled by Jesus that is necessary in order for the church to reflect in its life together the values and priorities of the kingdom of God. When this is the vision of pastoral care, then the practical concerns of counseling, visitation, and the rituals of Christian life are kept from being misunderstood as the essential work of pastors rather than properly understood as tools that pastors use to help keep the church attentive to God. This kind of view will open practices of pastoral care that include correction and discipline. Many contemporary pastors seem anxious to avoid these aspects of the work under the faulty belief that pastoral care has something to do with making people feel better. Seeking to help people feel better about themselves, or meeting people's needs (in the popularized sense of the phrase) is an unstable foundation from which to build a true pastoral ministry. This approach is rife with temptation to do the work in ways that make people happy or at the least to minimize criticism. My current role in the church as an overseer (*episkopos*) gives me a sad vantage point to the harm that is done in congregations when pastors see themselves as little more than spiritual cruise directors.

The Wesleys seemed far more interested in growing Christians than they were interested in pleasing people. The whole of their work bears witness that pastoral care has little to do with sentimentalized hand-holding and everything to do with guiding a people from love, through discipline, into the grace-enabled responses of Christlike obedience. If indeed pastoral care is about growing Christians, then what are some ways of doing this that find root not only in the Scriptures but also in Wesleyan theology and practice?

Care of the Whole

John Telford in *The Life of John Wesley* notes that "Wesley felt himself responsible for every side of his people's life. He was not content to be their adviser in spiritual matters only, but laboured to make them model citizens and subjects."[1] Holiness theology calls us to bring all of life under the Lordship of Jesus Christ. Wesley seemed to understand that this kind of Christian discipleship required the intentional engagement of pastors into all aspects of the lives of congregants. The pastoral care Wesley taught, modeled, and structured in the communal life of his revival movement reveals that he thought of pastoral care as much more than comforting people in their distress, although this is certainly part of the work. It also includes *discomforting* the people in terms of confession of sin, accountability for spiritual disciplines, and correction for errant belief or behavior, all placed against the rule of Scripture. In other words, a Wesleyan way of pastoral care is not content to reserve its work for the accepted venues of life where people are apt to desire the presence of a chaplain (e.g., funerals, weddings, hospitals, etc.). Rather, Wesleyan pastoral care is courageous (on the basis of biblical authority) to stick its nose into the business of people who may or may not be appreciative that we are calling them to wholehearted, whole-life embrace of "the upward call of God in Christ Jesus" (Phil. 3:14, ESV). Pastoral care under a Wesleyan paradigm must follow the people into their places of work, home, and play just as the Wesleys followed the people into the marketplaces, mines, and fields of England. John and Charles learned from their parents that Christian discipleship certainly speaks to citizenship and how one might, as a Christian, influence the policies and practices of the state. Some maintain that the Wesleyan revival may have spared England from the kind of bloody revolution experienced in France during the period because Methodists were continuously admonished to care for the oppressed lower classes. The point here being that a robust view of pastoral care must never allow it to become domesticated and assigned only to certain of life's concerns, but must be understood as *care for the whole*—the whole person and the whole community.

Rhythms of Spiritual Discipline

Wesleyan pastoral care takes place partly in response to events in the lives of people and in the community. However, Wesleyan pastoral care is not ordered only by reaction or response; it structures ministry with intention. One of the critiques of the Wesleys' early work was that they were "methodizing" spiritual life and growth. John and Charles understood something about the critical component of order in forming Christians. In contemporary Christianity the spiritual disciplines are too often conceived as individual and even private. One may first think of the disciplines of prayer, fasting, silence, and certainly solitude as individual and private. And yet even the meaning of a discipline like solitude is only fully realized in light of a community of Christians from which particular Christians periodically withdraw for the deeper works achieved in cell and desert. Wesleyan pastoral care would strike the *via media* (middle way) between asceticism and sensuality, not only calling people to know the range of spiritual disciplines but also providing systems for accountability (e.g., society, class, band) whereby pastoral care broadens from the office of pastor to the directed life of the community.

Pastoral care structures are also richly enhanced by the rhythms of the Christian year. The church measures time christologically by celebrating the events of Jesus' birth (Advent/Christmas), life and ministry (Epiphany), suffering and death (Lent), resurrection (Easter), and the outpouring of the Holy Spirit (Pentecost). John Westerhoff says that sharing a common memory and a common vision is what makes us a community. We "remain a community only insofar as [we tell] the story and live for the vision."[2] Time is a gift from God and is an important component in the shaping of mature believers. The manner in which pastors help the people mark time will have much to do with the spiritual health of congregations. The Christian calendar gives us wonderful opportunity for remembrance and preparation. It helps in special times to come away from the normal pursuits of life and rehearse the story of our redemption. These are practices that do much more than provide a reason to have events. These rhythmic practices of the Christian year provide careful pastors with rich resources for nurture and worship, which shape a people over time to recognize their identity as participants in the grand story of God.

Word and Table

Occasionally the conversations around pastoral practices might suggest that pastoral care is viewed as a set of tasks distinct from the central task of calling and guiding the people in worship. Because authentic pastoral care rises from the Word of God (first Jesus Christ and then the Scriptures) and the sacraments, the practices of the worshiping community become key components of faithful and effective pastoral care.

Preaching that is understood as more than instruction or inspiration but especially as spiritual formation provides a beautiful basis for the shared life of pastor and people. Unfortunately, contemporary preaching has too often been framed in terms of an inspirational talk or educational lecture. While each of these aspects is present in good preaching, they each fall short of a fuller idea of preaching as the loving work of a pastor who has given substantive time and energy to interpreting text and congregation with an eye always toward Sunday. The point of the work is not the study only, but that moment when the pastor has the blessed privilege of standing before the people under the authority of Christ Jesus to announce joyfully a word from the Lord. And it extends far beyond the worship gathering. This kind of pastoral preaching is never completed by the event of giving the sermon. Good pastoral preaching creates a congregational conversation that gives shape and substance to other acts of pastoral care, such as counseling, visitation, and discipling ministries. It can be at once gratifying and frightening for a preacher to realize that the people are actually making life decisions in response to the sermons! Biblical preaching that is carried by imaginative speech and anointed by the Holy Spirit is profound pastoral care.

Proclamation of the Word always moves toward response. This can include many different kinds of acts, such as prayer, confession, praise, and declaration. No act is more essential to Christian formation, however, than the act of coming to the table to receive with thanksgiving the gifts of bread and wine. Failure to provide this grace-enabled act of worship for the community of faith carefully and regularly is pastoral malpractice. The time and preparation that is required by pastors in order to set the table properly (in word and action) is a sacrificial gift of pastoral care. It requires theological precision and prayerful intention, recognizing that Christ is present in the Eucharist. It is memorial but it is far more. It is Communion, the sharing of life, a means of grace to the people of God.

One of the highlights of my pastoral ministry happened on my first Sunday back from a seven-week sabbatical. The service was ordered so that in response to the gospel I would have the privilege of looking each one of my congregants in the eye (nearly four hundred of them then) and calling them by name as I offered the elements saying, "The body and blood of our Lord given for you." It was much more than a moment, but a marker of seven previous years of life together and a milestone for seven more years of pastoral care that was created, ordered, and blessed by the poured-out life of Christ among us. Thanks be to God! Linking this back to the Wesleyan movement toward the margins, careful pastors insure that the consecrated elements are also distributed to those unable to come to the table in the worshiping community. Taking Communion to the infirm, homebound, and imprisoned is among the most precious of pastoral care works.

Prayer and Presence

The relational, love-oriented emphasis that is Wesleyan theology moves pastoral work out from the pulpit and altar into the homes and workplaces of the people. The ministry of the Wesleys was largely an itinerant ministry. Pastoral life is about "showing up" at the right moments in the lives of one's people—moments that are sometimes critical but often mundane. The itinerant work of John Wesley has in its core the conviction that the mission of God moves toward the people; it does not sit in one location and expect the people to come and receive. Recently a man who has been part of the church all of his life reported that to his memory, only once across several decades of Christian life did a pastor come to his workplace in order to ask the simple question, "How is it with your soul?" The business-style, CEO model of modern pastoral ministry deceived a generation into believing that pastors are too busy for such work. There is a deep need for pastors to become honest about what consumes their time. Technologies that can be wonderful tools for ministry can also become dangerous pits of wasted time and opportunity. Pastors should be careful about how much time they stay in their offices. You can't say that about a CEO! Wesleyan pastoral care gets out of the office and into the streets as a living sign of the in-breaking kingdom of God.

Careful pastors also know that just showing up is not all that is needed when we intersect the daily lives of our people. Our parishioners want to pray and very often they need help to pray. The pastor arrives at the bedside of one who is about to enter the hospital operating room not to offer anecdotes of similar experiences or divert the attention of the patient to other matters. We are there not only to pray over the patient but also to watch and pray with loved ones who await the result. The first time we handed over our baby boy to the surgeons we learned just how important it was to have our pastor there not only to comfort us by his very presence but especially to voice to God what we were not fully able to voice: a desperate cry for God's protecting and healing hand upon our son. Prayer is our first work and it is a great gift to offer prayer as a pastor alongside the people whom you love and serve. Much of the work of pastoral prayer, however, is done in the places of solitude where only eternity will fully reveal the loving work of pastors who faithfully call out the names of their people in prayer to God, not just during crises, but on an ongoing basis.

One other component of pastoral presence that deserves mention here is the commitment to remain with a people to whom one has been called. The classical vows of ordination had to do with poverty, chastity, and obedience. William Willimon notes that in the sixth century Saint Benedict added to these three core promises a fourth, "the vow of stability, the vow to remain where God had placed you, to persist in community, even when the community did not please you personally, to develop the disciplines required to remain where God wanted you to be."[3] Some of the dis-ease that is present in congregations today falls squarely at the feet of pastors who apparently view the relationship of pastor and people as more *contractual* than *covenantal*. I hear pastors regularly justify leaving their congregations with the language of "feeling released" from the assignment. Certainly God may release one from a particular assignment, but this is a matter of careful and prayerful discernment best navigated within the counsel of leaders in the church. The pressure points at which pastors are tempted to retreat are often the very moments when significant ministry is emerging, because pastors work at the dangerous intersection of the kingdom of God with the kingdoms of this world. Rich pastoral care may be realized right at the point of collision, difficult as it is to walk through those times.

Wesleyan Pastoral Care

Pastoral care is best accomplished in a Wesleyan theological framework because this paradigm provides the most helpful ways to structure ministry so that it reflects the work of a God who loves "with an everlasting love" (Jer. 31:3). A Wesleyan understanding of grace offers the pastor a capacity to love consistently a people who are consistently difficult to love. A Wesleyan understanding of faith offers the pastor the gifts of optimism and hope that the "now and not yet" Kingdom is coming in the work of our crucified and risen Lord. And a Wesleyan understanding of holiness offers the pastor the confidence that truly there is enough power in the death and resurrection of Jesus actually to transform a person's life and to enable us, by grace, to live Christlike lives in this world. Pastors get to lead the way on behalf of a God "who always leads us in triumphal procession in Christ and through us spreads everywhere the fragrance of the knowledge of him" (2 Cor. 2:14).

Discussion Questions

1. Why do you think the church throughout its history finds it wise to set aside some of its members to the life and work of pastoral ministry?

2. The idea of pastor is imaged in the work of a shepherd. What are some ways that the image of a shepherd informs the life and work of a pastor in the church?

3. Is it possible that congregations might become complicit in tempting pastors to divert from the core of their work? What are some ways this might happen and how could a congregation protect against such diversions?

4. While we are most familiar and perhaps most comfortable with the pastoral works of mercy, comfort, and teaching, pastors are also called to exhort, correct, even discipline the people of God. How open are contemporary Christians to these aspects of pastoral leadership?

Recommended Reading

Hansen, D. *The Art of Pastoring: Ministry Without All the Answers.* Downers Grove, IL: InterVarsity Press, 1994.

Peterson, Eugene H. *Working the Angles: The Shape of Pastoral Integrity.* Grand Rapids: Eerdmans, 1987.

Purves, A. *Pastoral Theology in the Classical Tradition.* Louisville, KY: Westminster John Knox Press, 2001.

Rowell, Jeren. *What's a Pastor to Do? The Good and Difficult Work of Ministry.* Kansas City: Beacon Hill Press of Kansas City, 2004.

Willimon, William. *Pastor, the Theology and Practice of Ordained Ministry.* Nashville: Abingdon Press, 2002.

six

STANDING IN THE GAP
WESLEYAN FOUNDATIONS FOR PASTORAL COUNSELING

Glena Andrews

Pastors are in a unique position. They guide their congregation through more public ministries but are considered by members of their church, neighborhood, and larger community to be resources during times of personal or private trouble. A church organization may have educational classes, programs for food and clothing distribution, Bible studies, addiction recovery programs, and other such ministries, but the pastor will still be viewed as the person in whom to confide during times of relational, emotional, and psychological difficulties. It is at this point that the preaching pastor, the program pastor, or the administration pastor becomes the counseling pastor.

During the introduction to my Abnormal Psychology class, I suggest a variety of professionals who would benefit in their chosen career from learning the information of this course, including the expected careers of counseling, psychiatry, and social work, and I always include ministers. I receive curious looks from the students questioning why a religion or ministry major should take a class about mental illness. I ask how many of my students would go to a counselor, psychologist, social worker, or psychiatrist first if they found themselves struggling with serious sadness or anxiety, if they were unable to stop a destructive behavior, or were the victim of an assault. A few hands go up. Next I ask the students to raise their hand if they would meet with their pastor or youth pastor before ever walking into the office of a mental health professional. At least twice as many hands will be raised in response. As our discussion proceeds, exploring why the students would go to their pastor first, the myths about people with mental illness begin to be revealed; the belief that Christians should rely on God only is voiced along with the suggestion that a person with mental health issues has a weak relationship with God. Many stereotypes about mental health professionals are expressed. The idea that a pastor is often the first person seen by people with mental health difficulties becomes very clear, and then I ask my students why ministry and religion majors are not required to take Abnormal Psychology. There are many responses, including that they don't need to know about mental disorders to help people; ministry majors get the necessary information in their theology classes; and God will guide them when the time comes. Most of my students are Christians, so I pose the question to them; why are you in the class? Won't God guide you when the time comes? The classroom is often quiet at this point, and I take the opportunity to stress that it is critical that people in all types of ministry be familiar with symptoms of mental illness, addictions, complicated bereavement, signs of suicidal ideation, and other issues related to mental health challenges. It is important to have an understanding of what behaviors, thoughts, feelings, and emotions are a result of normal reactions to daily stress and at what point the person crossed over into symptoms that suggest a more serious issue. Requirements for an education in basic mental illness or even basic counseling skills are not always a reality for most educational programs designed for people considering a career in ministry, thus chapters such as this one can be helpful if not crucial.

The phrase "pastoral counseling" can refer to any situation in which a person in a ministry position is listening, supporting, consoling, or advising an individual within his or her church congregation. Or it can refer to the formal title and profession of pastoral counselor. The second is a person with specific training in theology and counseling who has completed degrees and licensing exams. This person may or may not be in an official ministry position with the church or a para-church organization. The focus of this chapter is to consider the first instance, specifically exploring an understanding of counseling methods that are in harmony with a Wesleyan theological perspective that are helpful for the pastor when a person comes into the office and seeks "counsel" or "counseling."

The Need for Networks and Community

For the same reasons that no psychologist, social worker, psychiatrist, or counselor should see himself or herself as able to address all problems in society, a pastor should never see himself or herself having the skills or knowledge to address all mental health and relationship issues. It is important to have resources for mental health situations, including appropriate contacts for emergency situations, local police numbers, contacts to report child, elder, and domestic abuse, and referral information for mental health professionals. Developing relationships with professionals such as police personnel who investigate domestic violence, social workers who work with child protective services, counselors specializing in addictions recovery or family counseling, psychologists who work with assessing learning disabilities or provide services for those with severe mental illness, and physicians or psychiatrists who manage medications can all be extremely valuable during times when referrals need to be made. Psychologists, professional counselors, and ministers can develop working relationships that are beneficial to the client who is struggling to overcome mental health issues, especially when a holistic perspective is a shared value.

Using a Holistic View of Humankind

A Wesleyan theological perspective of counseling provides the minister with a structure that is founded on a holistic view of all humankind. Critical to a Wesleyan view of the nature of humans is the understanding that to be the persons God created us to become we must be seen as beings designed to be in relationship with God, and the understanding that this relationship is one bathed in love. The underlying foundation is that God created human beings as essentially good. With this foundation the pastor is able to look beyond the behavior, the troubled thoughts, or the troubled spirit to see the person God created. This view of an individual can be the beginning of healing. When persons have been severely damaged by the world and/or their own poor choices, it can be difficult to believe in their underlying goodness. During the process of working toward health, of peeling back the barriers, opening wounds for healing or facing harsh realities about oneself, it sometimes requires the counselor to carry the belief of inherent goodness for the person. Wesley's belief that personal involvement with God is critical and dynamic is a beneficial view for working with people. As the pastor listens, he or she becomes involved in a relationship with the congregant that is dynamic and interactive. The minister can share how God desires to be in relationship with us. It is this personal dimension of God's desire to be in relationship with us that is critical and is what distinguished holiness theology from a more pessimistic theology of humanity for John Wesley.[1]

Multifaceted Nature of Humankind

John Wesley was concerned with multiple aspects of human life. The spiritual condition of a person was critical, but Wesley used multiple methods for living out his calling to minister to God's people. He was involved in social justice, helped those who were in poverty, counseled to mental health needs, and even diagnosed and treated physical illness.[2] The business of ministering to people was not solely about preaching and teaching people that they were sinners in need of repentance. Mildred Bangs Wynkoop gives us a list of activities in which John Wesley involved himself that were considered outside the realm of clergy in Wesley's time, including writing a "four-volume *History of England*," "writing a medical book, setting up a free medical dispensary, adapting an electrical machine for healing," and "setting up spinning and knitting shops for the poor."[3] It is not expected that the local pastor take on the role of physician, historian, pharmacist, and entrepreneur, but Wesley's example suggests that we are to look at the person in his or her environment; the child within the family, the spouse within the marriage, the individual within the home and work environment, and the family within the community. It suggests that we see the person as a child of God, loved by God, with physical, spiritual, mental, and emotional abilities and needs.

In a holistic view, as one element is changed, it affects all elements. The adolescent who is struggling with handling peer pressure cannot be empowered to be strong without that change in thinking and behavior affecting peer relationships, family dynamics, and personal perspective. Thus when the pastor is listening to an adult who is so anxious that he or she is unable to function outside the home or within the family, it is important to see the person as connected through multiple relationships to family, church, and community. Change and healing can begin in various places, but any change will affect all relationships for this person. A pastor must be very discerning. When a person is homeless or in a violent situation, drudging up past or present abuse memories is not appropriate and can actually cause additional trauma. Meeting the person at his or her current needs is more therapeutic—such as finding stable housing, employment, or finishing an educational program. These methods may not feel like counseling, but they are necessary in order for deeper healing to be effective.

A Wesleyan Foundation for Counseling: The Quadrilateral

The pillars of the Wesleyan quadrilateral can be a beneficial structure for a pastor counseling a congregant. Finding tools through Scripture, tradition, experience, and reason can help the minister to set appropriate goals for guiding the parishioner toward health and healing. The understanding of how *Scripture* informs us of God's amazing love for us can be used to provide support and encouragement for a person who is struggling with emotional distress and daily stress reactions. Wesley was constantly faithful to view all aspects of his ministry and his instruction through the lens of Scripture. He thoughtfully looked at Scripture within context and avoided using specific verses outside of the proper context. It can be tempting to use a verse of Scripture to try to teach or console a person, but unless the meaning of the verse is understood within appropriate context it can result in harmful consequences. God and Scripture should not be used as a tool to intimidate or shame a person seeking counsel. But there are appropriate times for using prayer and Bible reading to strengthen a person's faith and empower the person to make difficult decisions and act on them. The Wesleyan perspective of viewing the person holistically will enable the pastor to incorporate prayer and Scripture into the counseling sessions with an understanding of the person's strengths, afflictions, and potential.

Healthy, appropriate *tradition,* as defined by Wesleyan theology, can provide rich examples of appropriate pathways that a person can use to approach difficult situations. From tradition we not only have doctrinal foundations but also have examples of the healing energy of community, the uplifting support from small groups of people seeking God, and the freeing experiences that can come through faithful and respectful communication. John Wesley respected people of various Christian traditions.[4] His concern was whether the person's heart was "right with God" rather than what church or denomination held his or her membership.[5] In the same way individuals who walk into the pastor's office may not hold membership in the pastor's specific church or any church but can be connected to services and resources sponsored by the church.

Reason can be beneficial for helping a person move beyond the emotional and develop a cognitive structure for facing daily struggles, especially those situations that cannot be changed, such as illness, injury, or the death of a loved one. Often people who are struggling with symptoms of mental illness or involved in unhealthy relationships have a sense of what choice to make but do not have the internal power or confidence to make those choices. For example, a young adult who is suffering with panic and anxiety "knows" that his or her reaction is irrational but may not have the courage to face the challenge that underlies the cause of the anxiety. Listening actively to his or her fears of applying for employment, saying something embarrassing at the interview or on a date can lead to empowering the young adult to explore the anxieties within the supportive environment of the pastor's office, accepting the support from a caring believer, and thinking through appropriate scenarios that would lead to success and decreased anxiety.

Often persons who suffer from depression and anxiety can hold to a "false self." Helping people face their false self can enable them to become free from faulty thinking (which can affect their emotions), destructive relationships, from unhealthy or false "love." It can be difficult to understand these distortions without the opportunity to talk to another person who has skills to listen, assess, and direct the individual to carefully look at dysfunctional behaviors. A person who struggles with relationship after relationship may believe that it is the other persons who ruin the relationships. He or she may fail to understand how, for example, constant criticism of others (arising from personal insecurity or from an exaggerated sense of self) contributes to the poor relationship. Taking responsibility for our actions is key. Or, in another example, persons who are addicted to behaviors or substances may deny that these have control over them and negatively affect relationships. The first step in change is clarity of thought about oneself. In these situations caring but straight confrontation may be helpful, even necessary, to the healing of the individual and the individual's relationships. Persons who have incorrect thinking about themselves, once they gain insight, are going to need support and encouragement to continue to face the truth.

Experience can provide rich learning opportunities for many people. Experience is where we can "touch" each other, engage with one another, and find the personal experience of healing. Healthy experience can be helpful to encourage people and provide them with a way to move from rumination or unhealthy thinking to using their energy toward positive action. Research in psychology has demonstrated that when a person begins to act in positive and healthy ways, symptoms of anxiety and depression can be reduced. Certainly faith can help a person "existentially."

Wesleyan theology especially emphasizes the relational and the personal.[6] A "person is body and mind, heart and spirit, conscience and will."[7] According to Wynkoop,

> Personal relationship becomes a reality when two selves . . . open themselves to each other, respect the moral autonomy of each other, honor the personal integrity of each other, esteem each other as they esteem themselves, share themselves with each other without demanding mindless capitulation from each other, and then respond to each other in the profound awareness of mutual intercommunication. In this encounter which defines fellowship, the integrity of each is maintained and enhanced without the surrender of anything essential to selfhood.[8]

Understanding these principles and using them in the counseling relationship enables the pastor to model healthy relationships. As the individual tells his or her story—revealing poor choices and discussing inappropriate or destructive behavior—the pastor enters into genuine relationship. Through this relationship the minister is able to model respect and communication skills, demonstrate appropriate personal boundaries, and provide a safe place where the individual can move toward healing. The experience of entering into a healthy, appropriate, and safe relationship can teach the congregant lessons about what a healthy relationship feels and looks like and provide a place where he or she can practice being a person in a dynamic, personal, and appropriate relationship.

Client-Centered Therapy Tools

One of the most popular counseling techniques used today comes from the theories of Carl Rogers, a psychologist who developed client-centered therapy.[9] These techniques are often the first methods taught to students pursuing a counseling profession, and include active listening, unconditional positive regard (i.e., love), and empowering the person to find internal strength to make changes. Rogers believed each person to be responsible for his or her choices and proposed that the "therapist" is not the expert but rather is joining with the client to support the client toward health.

One of the most helpful techniques from client- or person-centered therapy is to listen and let people know you are listening. This tool is called active listening.[10] We feel valued when we are heard. But active listening can be more difficult than first imagined. Oftentimes people in positions of support or authority fall into a habit of listening just long enough to think they know what the issue is that the client or parishioner is trying to express. Then they jump in to "help" and give advice to the person. This action invalidates the person and sets up a hierarchy of power suggesting the parishioner is incapable of understanding the problem, powerless to make a change, or unable to find an appropriate solution. Active listening requires the pastor to listen and verify that he or she has fully understood by reflecting back what is being heard. Using the phrase, "What I think I hear you saying is . . ." is an effective way of letting the person know you are listening and have heard correctly. If you have misunderstood, the person is then able to respond and correct the misunderstanding. A pastor has the opportunity to listen and to understand without assuming he or she "knows the problem." Many times people who are struggling with emotional distress or mental health issues already feel fear or shame. To have a person truly listen and work to understand while avoiding cliché advice is powerful and can begin the process of healing and trust.

Sin and Responsibility

Sinful behavior is not glossed over or ignored by those with a Wesleyan perspective, but the sin does not define the person. Wesley did not excuse people from being responsible for their actions. People are "responsible down to the core of [their] being and in this responsibility relates . . . to God and [people]."[11] Wesley did not adhere to the concept that people should grovel or undervalue themselves. He understood that human beings were fallible and struggled with weaknesses.[12] He did not see physical and emotional problems as spiritual problems as some do. People cannot heal themselves and are not gods. When we lose the understanding of God as love and humankind of the recipients of that love, we lose perspective.

The tool of unconditional positive regard proposed by Rogers directs the counselor to help to create an environment in which the person senses a safe place in which he or she is able to explore struggles without judgments. This does not suggest that the negative, hurtful, or destructive behaviors are ignored or the person engages in blaming others for his or her choices, but rather the person is accepted as a creation of God with value, who is loved by God, while learning to alter behaviors, thoughts, or emotions (with God's grace). Unconditional positive regard suggests that the person is valued while the problems are addressed.

What does a pastor who is counseling do about sin? Often parishioners come to talk as a means of catharsis or "confession." In the tone of the Wesleyan tradition, "original sin" does not need to be ignored when working with people. Wesley does not consider that original sin would cause a person to be without hope[13] nor that people were destined for eternal damnation by original sin alone. Sin is a "voluntary transgression of a known law of God."[14] He stresses that each person must know he or she is damaged and in a sense corrupt, and that salvation is the healing, even the destruction of sin.

The pastor has the opportunity to encourage the person to seek salvation, believe in God's love, and understand that the holiness God calls us to is rooted in our personal communion and deep fellowship with God. God desires our love and gives love; grace is always God reaching out to humankind. A person who is suffering from depression may need to be reminded of this powerful love and that he or she is a recipient of this love and of salvation.

There are times when a person seems to be unable to move beyond rumination or compulsive complaining. The person's ability to reason, to find the core of the issue by talking, may be impaired. At these times using tools from cognitive-behavioral therapy is helpful; aiding the person in changing his or her behaviors (e.g., getting out of the house) and thoughts can help move the person beyond the symptoms. With cognitive-behavioral techniques, the reason behind the symptoms is not as important as the behavior or thoughts that lead to the expression of the symptoms. But Wesleyan theology affirms that God can help us develop new ways of thinking as God gives us "the mind of Christ."

Responsibility Beyond the Self

With personal freedom comes personal responsibility, "to be free is to be responsible."[15] Trying to be a person different from one's own true self robs us of freedom. Even with a foundation of goodness, people are not designed to be isolated or to be completed with only a relationship with God. With personal freedom comes personal responsibility, "to be free is to be responsible." To be a person requires being in relationships and being aware of self, in the true sense, demands an awareness of others. We are to be in community with other individuals. Wesleyans view people as social beings who are foundational in their view. Holiness did not separate people from one another. Holiness for John Wesley was "social holiness."[16]

Loving God with our whole being and our neighbors as ourselves is definitive of holiness for Wesleyans. And in a sense holiness is about being free to love. But there are situations in which a person has been so damaged by this world through destructive relationships that he or she is not able to make appropriate choices. Sometimes a person has no confidence in making any choices and thus allows others to choose for him or her. This will lead to symptoms of depression and anxiety and an unhealthy dependence on others. This person is technically "in relationship" with others, but not in the way God intended. According to Wesley self-love is necessary before we can love others.[17] But many persons are estranged from themselves. This can cause a feeling of isolation, self-hate, and insecurity. The person is dependent on others to make decisions but is unable to love himself or herself and thus cannot really love others. In this situation there really is no relationship. When this is understood it is a very frightening concept. The Wesleyan perspective insists that we must have self-acceptance and self-esteem. Isolation and alienation is a "description of sin."[18] Love of self, as God intended is not selfishness nor self-focus. It is a deep appreciation for who God has created each person to become.

At the same time a person is learning to love himself or herself, the person is also developing healthy relationships. This is necessary for healing. Wesley taught that the stronger our fellowship with others, the stronger the self. It is important to model this type of community in the counseling relationship, but also to encourage the person to developing healthy and whole relationships within the community. Personal healing and relational healing bring wholeness. And wholeness is intricately interconnected with holiness, the heart of the Wesleyan message.

Discussion Questions

1. Why does the author suggest that pastors are in a unique position when considering counseling?

2. The author suggests some reasons why people might choose to talk with a pastor about mental health or relationships issues before seeking help from a professional mental health worker. What are some other reasons a pastor is sought out first?

3. What are some issues that it would make "looking beyond the behavior" of a person difficult? How can a pastor use counseling skills to aid in seeing the person rather than the behavior?

4. John Wesley seemed to become whatever was necessary to meet the needs of the people. Should pastors also see their role this way or is today different? Why?

5. What are some of the challenges in working with people with emotional and mental health issues in terms of sin?

Recommended Reading

Collins, Gary R. *Helping People.* Ventura, CA: Vision House, 1982.

Rogers, Carl, and Peter D. Kramer. *On Becoming a Person: A Therapist's View of Psychotherapy.* New York: Mariner Books, 1995.

Sanders, Randolph K. *Christian Counseling Ethics: A Handbook for Therapists, Pastors, and Counselors.* Grand Rapids: InterVarsity Press, 1997.

Townsend, Loren. *Introduction to Pastoral Counseling.* Nashville: Abingdon Press, 2009.

Wynkoop, Mildred Bangs. *A Theology of Love.* Kansas City: Beacon Hill Press of Kansas City, 1972.

seven

FILLING THE BUCKET
A WESLEYAN WAY TO CARE FOR YOURSELF AND THE ONES YOU LOVE

~~⌇~~

Michael Pitts

Do all the good you can, by all the means you can, in all the ways you can,
in all the places you can, at all the times you can,
to all the people you can, as long as ever you can.[1]

There is a two-pronged emphasis in this well-known quote of John Wesley's: (1) Do all the good you can, (2) to all the people you can. The rest of the quote focuses on how, where, and when we can do this.

"Do all the good you can . . ." is actually an invitation to express genuine love, since for Wesley only a person who acts out of love is really doing good.[2] However, "There is something within us that knows that love is more than what we think or even what we do. We recognize that love includes affect."[3] First Corinthians 13, the love chapter, provides clear descriptors of the affect that is at the heart of love. Love delights and rejoices. Love protects, trusts, and hopes. Love is kind and others-oriented. In Wesleyan thought, then, doing "good" is evidenced by heartfelt loving action.

". . . to all the people you can . . ." When reading this phrase many of us are likely to think broadly in terms of who "all the people" are—like the huddled masses, the poor, perhaps even congregations. However, the full scope of this phrase compels us to consider *all* people. Who

are these people? Well, among others, you are people. Your spouse and your children are people. So, built into the Wesley Rule is a mandate to care for ourselves and those in our family. As Scripture reminds us, "Each of you should look *not only* to your own interests, but also to the interests of others" (Phil. 2:4, italics added).

There are studies showing that a pastor's ability to serve others effectively is totally dependent on his or her ability to function and be healthy.[4] In other words, without self-care, the care of others becomes more and more difficult. Flight attendants say it this way: "In case of an emergency, place your own oxygen mask on before helping others." Even the airlines acknowledge the relationship between self-care and care of others.

"Wesley recognized four basic human relationships: with God, with other humans, with lower animals, and with ourselves. A holy (and whole!) person is one in whom all of these relationships are properly expressed. When each of these relationships is properly expressed, we will also have a proper relationship to ourselves of self-acceptance."[5] Once again, we see that, for Wesley, there is an important relationship between self-care and care of others.

Most pastors would agree, at least in theory, that to be healthy there must be a balance of self-care as well as care for the primary relationships in their lives—the family. Some studies have shown, however, that it is easier for those in ministry to give than to receive. When giving is done to excess, it can result in a slow and sure depletion of healthy inner resources.[6] Finding the balance and keeping self-care and family care moving in the right direction is an ongoing challenge for every pastor.

The Starting Point for Self-Care and Family Care

An old Chinese proverb reads, "Unless we change directions we are likely to end up where we are headed."[7] This proverb holds the potential for good news or bad news—depending on the current direction

87

of your personal and family life. If it's good news, stay the course. If it's bad news, consider the following questions and others like them, as a means of changing your direction:

1. If I woke up tomorrow morning and my _____ (spiritual, emotional, physical, mental) life was headed in the direction I want to be going, what would I be doing that I am currently not doing?

2. What does my spouse need from me that I am not currently providing?

3. Do I need to do something different regarding the amount of time and attention I am giving to my children? If so, what?

4. What can I do *today* to implement the answers to these questions?

Self-Care

There is a story of a lumberjack in the days when trees were cut by hand and salary was determined by the number of trees cut. On Monday and Tuesday the lumberjack cut down eight trees each day. He decided he could earn more money by getting up earlier and cutting a tree before breakfast. He did, and on Wednesday he cut down nine trees. On Thursday, he skipped breakfast in order to cut down an additional tree. However, by the end of the day he had only cut down eight trees. Intent on increasing his productivity on Friday, he cut down an extra tree after dark instead of resting. When he tallied his output for the day he totaled only seven trees. On Saturday he kept the same hours but injured his foot while cutting after dark. Saturday's output—six trees. He was so intent on being productive that he didn't take time to see the doctor, but believed he could still increase his output for the week by working on Sunday. Sunday morning found him exhausted, hungry, lonely for his friends, and his foot was hurting. On Sunday he cut down five trees. On Monday morning he went to see his foreman to tell him he was not cut out to be a lumberjack. He quit his job and went home.[8]

This story illustrates an important truth for lumberjacks—and pastors. The self has limits. We cannot continually add to our schedules and demands without an eventual decrease in effectiveness and productivity. How many pastors have walked into the foreman's office to say "I'm done"?

In one of his sermons, John Wesley reminds us that, "faith does not overturn the course of nature."[9] A call to ministry is not a gift of a Kevlar-coated life. We can't live on less sleep, and we are not somehow stronger in all dimensions of our humanity simply because we are serving in a pastoral role. Our strength comes the same way it comes to everyone else—by paying attention to the details of what it means to be a human being. The following suggestions are a few ways to pay attention to those details.

1. Take "the Temple" Concept Seriously

"Do you not know that your body is a temple of the Holy Spirit, who is in you, whom you have received from God? You are not your own; you were bought at a price. Therefore honor God with your body" (1 Cor. 6:19-20). Self-care is good stewardship. Yet, one of the main barriers pastors face regarding personal health is the tendency to "put everyone else's needs before their own and to have unrealistically high expectations for themselves."[10] To be healthy, however, we have to pay attention to self-care. If we ignore any dimension of the "self" God created, we put ourselves and those around us at a disadvantage.

- *Care for your spirit:* In addition to the Scripture, read classic devotional books for your own growth. Pray about your journey, reflect on your relationship with Christ, and meditate on the work of the Holy Spirit in you. Make time to be alone for rest, reflection, and renewal.

- *Care for your body:* There are two areas where pastors seem to be less healthy than the general population—diet and exercise.[11] Give your body the attention it deserves. There is nothing that can replace the need for adequate sleep, healthy eating, and appropriate exercise. Wesley, when writing to pastors about caring for the body, penned these words: "Let nothing hinder you. Your life is at stake. Make everything yield to this."[12]

- *Care for your mind:* Just like your body, your mind needs exercise. Renew your mind through prayer and contemplation. Stimulate your mind through what you read. Relax your mind through developing a hobby and making time for fun.

- *Care for your emotions:* It is important for us to understand our emotions since prolonged emotional exhaustion results in ineffective ministry.[13] Learn the causes of your joy and sadness, your relaxation and stress, and your sense of calm and anxiety. Then commit your emotional life to God and seek the help of his Spirit in finding emotional balance. If family and close friends are not able to assist you in dealing with feelings appropriately, seek the help of your family physician or a professional counselor.

2. Decide on *What You Will Not Tolerate*

Dr. Viktor Frankl, the founder of Logotherapy, was fond of telling how, in the later years of his life, he developed a fear of flying. Each time he boarded a plane his anxiety increased. He decided to counteract his fear of boarding commercial airliners by taking flying lessons and obtaining his pilot's license. When a friend quizzed him about this he responded, "You know, there are some things about yourself you just don't have to tolerate."[14] For Viktor Frankl, it was a fear of flying. What might it be for you? Is there an attitude, a habit, or a behavior that you need to examine? Is there anything about the way you are living that makes you uncomfortable? If so, how long are you willing to tolerate it?

3. Be Willing to Seek Help

"Let us consider how we may spur one another on toward love and good deeds" (Heb. 10:24). Who in your life spurs you on? The Lone

Ranger had Tonto, and you need someone too. We all need someone who knows us well enough and loves us strongly enough to say, "I am concerned about you and here is why I am concerned."

Surveys report that 70 percent of pastors do not have someone they consider a close friend.[15] Living in isolation is a formula for disaster. Almost every pastor who experiences moral failure in ministry has lived some important aspect of life in isolation. Make sure you are building accountability friendships and seeking qualified professional help if life becomes unmanageable.

Family Care

At a meeting of ministers one pastor announced that he had decided to leave his church and the ministry. He had concluded that he could not be a pastor as well as father and husband. Furthermore, he was beginning to think the Catholics had the right idea. Ministry was so full-time that there was no room for other relational commitments, and he was unwilling to lead that kind of life. While that level of commitment to ministry may be the illusion some pastors live under, it is not the calling of God or the church.

Nurturing your relationships with your spouse and your children is not only healthy and healing but also scriptural. When it comes to giving yourself to others, put your family at the top of the list.

The following suggestions could revolutionize some family relationships:

1. Everyone Has a Dipper—Use Yours to Fill Buckets

Each one of us has an invisible bucket that is constantly emptied or filled, depending on what others say or do to us. When our bucket is full, we feel great. When it's empty, we feel awful. Each of us also has an invisible dipper that we use to fill other people's buckets by saying or doing things to increase their positive feelings about themselves. However, when we use our dipper to dip from someone else's bucket by saying or doing things that decrease their positive emotions, we diminish them. Every drop *in* a bucket makes us stronger and more optimistic about ourselves, our circumstances, and about life. Every drop *out* of our bucket saps our energy and undermines our self-concept. So, we face a choice every moment of every day: We can fill each other's buckets—or we can dip from them. It is an important choice—one that profoundly influences our relationships, productivity, health, and happiness.[16] Fill the buckets of people in your congregation—but save your biggest dipper for your spouse and your children.

2. Create Family Space in Your Life

"If anyone does not provide for his relatives, and especially for his immediate family, he has denied the faith and is worse than an unbeliever" (1 Tim. 5:8). Consider two thoughts: (1) "anyone" means anyone—including pastors, and (2) the term "provide" means much more than simply meeting physical needs.

One of the most important ways you can provide for your spouse and children is to give them your time. We can create what Henri Nouwen calls a voluntary space in our lives—a voluntary poverty of mind and heart that opens up an empty space of hospitality to receive the thoughts and feelings and experiences of others.[17]

You can create family space in your life by prioritizing time with your spouse and family. It can help to regularly schedule time on the calendar just like other appointments that are a priority for ministry rather than giving time to family as the busyness of ministry allows.

Regarding your spouse—consider the following: Put date nights on your calendar. Come home early once in a while just to go on a walk together. Hold hands often and create space in your lives to remind each other of what first attracted you to one another. Grow in your knowledge and understanding of how your spouse interprets expressions of love. We don't all speak the same love language. Become proficient at your spouse's language.[18]

Regarding your children—a survey of fifteen-year-olds revealed what they were looking for in the adults in their lives. Here are their top ten tips for developing positive relationships:

1. Look at us
2. Spend time talking with us
3. Listen
4. Be dependable
5. Show appreciation for what we do
6. Relax
7. Show that you're interested
8. Laugh with us (and at yourself)
9. Ask us to help you
10. Challenge us[19]

The actions on this list could improve any relationship. Putting these tips into practice with your own children could make a positive difference in your family life.

3. Listen Actively

As pointed out in the last chapter, most pastors receive much more training in how to speak than they do in how to listen. Listening is what we are doing when we aren't talking. Right? Well, no. The moment we are forming a response, we are no longer fully listening at home. When we are reading the paper during a conversation, we are not fully listening. Watching a ball game or listening to the news while a family member is talking to us is a sure sign that we are not fully listening. No matter how skilled we might be a multitasking, true listening calls for full and undivided attention.

One of the best ways to communicate your full attention is through what is known as SOLER listening.

Squarely facing the person you are talking to insures a better overall communication

Open body posture communicates acceptance of the content

Leaning into the conversation emotionally and physically communicates investment

Eye contact tells the other you are focused on him or her

Relaxed in posture and attitude suggests you are at ease with this person[20]

SOLER listening—like solar power—it's a great way to energize these relationships by warming up and empowering your family.

Conclusion

Pastors who live a life of always responding to the needs of others at the expense of their own needs or the needs of their family are driven by a demanding schedule that can result in exhaustion and burnout. It is not God's intention that we deplete ourselves and/or our families for the sake of everyone else we minister to. While our theological heritage compels us to "do all the good we can . . . to all the people we can," it also calls us to a balance in life that is characterized by love and care for self and family. This love is expressed through our thoughts, our feelings, and our actions. By the grace of God and with the help of the Holy Spirit, we can live this life.

Make deliberate choices to do the right thing—take care of yourself and take care of your family. Your life and well-being, and the life and well-being of your family, is at stake. Make everything yield to this.

Discussion Questions

1. Considering your body as the temple of the Holy Spirit, which dimension of your being needs the most attention—spirit, body, mind, emotions? What do you need to do to take care of each dimension of your life? What can you do now that will begin to make a difference?

2. "There are some things about yourself you just don't have to tolerate." When thinking about Viktor Frankl's statement, what is the first thing that comes to mind? What needs to be done to bring about change in this area of your life?

3. If you are currently serving as a Lone Ranger, name three people you could approach as accountability/prayer partners. Commit to developing a caring/sharing relationship with at least one of them. If you have someone you share your life with, renew the commitment to openness and honesty.

4. Keep track of positive and negative comments you make to family members for a day or a week. Are you filling their buckets or are you emptying them? Make a decision to do or say something today that will pour from your dipper into every family member's bucket.

5. Make a list of things you can do to create more family space in your life. Which will you do first?

6. How well do you put SOLER listening into practice? What might need to change for you to communicate your full attention to family members?

Recommended Reading

Chapman, Gary. *The Five Love Languages.* Chicago: Northfield Publishing, 1995.

Frankl, Viktor E. *Man's Search for Meaning.* New York: Simon and Schuster, 1959.

Nouwen, Henri J. M. *The Wounded Healer.* New York: Doubleday, 1972.

Peterson, Eugene H. *Working the Angles: The Shape of Pastoral Integrity.* Grand Rapids: Eerdmans, 1987.

Rath, Tom, and Donald Clifton. *How Full Is Your Bucket?* New York: Gallup Press, 2005.

Smalley, Gary. *Love Is a Decision*. Irving, TX: Word Publishing, 1989.

Wright, H. Norman. *The Secrets of a Lasting Marriage*. Ventura, CA: Regal Books, 1995.

eight

LEADING WITH BASIN AND TOWEL
SERVANT LEADERSHIP IN A WESLEYAN FRAMEWORK

Ed Robinson

There were eras when pastoral leadership seemed like a simple endeavor. It was simple, not easy. A pastor's "calling" was to preach (always first on the list, whether or not it happened to be a strength), pray, read the Bible, talk with most anyone about spiritual things without worrying if it might offend someone, provide spiritual care and comfort when people were in need, care for the church property (which, in many instances, had been in the same location for decades and was pasture for many "sacred cows"), encourage laity to lead quality programs for children and youth, and support the missionaries with monthly society meetings and special offerings.

The pastor had a "study" not an "office." Few people came to the church building for anything but regularly scheduled services because they knew that eventually the pastor would call on them or, in the case of an emergency, was only a phone call away. The pastor cherished opportunities to be present at parishioners' important family events like births, dedications, baptisms, marriages, and funerals (particularly of the saints). Parishioners regularly invited pastors (and their families) for dinner (except on Saturday night, of course) because it was an honor to have the minister "grace" their homes.

Pastoral life wasn't completely serene. There were midnight calls for crisis care, intense weeks (not days) of revival services, tiring all-day sessions of Vacation Bible School, church workdays for routine maintenance, and the annual vote of the congregation to determine whether she gets to keep her mailing address for another year. It was hard but rewarding work and almost everyone, saint and sinner alike, considered it a noble calling.

The times have changed and so has pastoring. It is still hard work, but it is anything but simple. I just finished reading a book manuscript of a pastoral colleague who was trying to make sense of his experience serving with vision in a congregation with sometimes competing agendas among its leadership. The church was rooted in its denominational programs and parallel currents of contemporary expressions within the larger stream of Wesleyan-holiness theology. Efforts to forge creative ministries outside of the mainstream were met with caution and, at times, explicit resistance. Attempts at casting vision and institutional "change" were viewed as disruptive at best or subversively manipulative at worst. Some who wanted change and applauded the pastoral initiatives left because the changes didn't happen fast enough. Some who resisted change left because what they projected for their future wasn't in keeping with what they wanted in a church. My friend chose to leave for the sake of the church's future by giving the congregation an opportunity for a fresh start with new pastoral leadership. In the end, allies and enemies and pastor went packing. Amid the challenges, the church still had services every Sunday morning, Sunday evening, and Wednesday night. They continue to support denominational initiatives. Those who are left continued to give tithes and offerings. The church will survive, but the congregation lost most of the momentum it had been garnering for a couple of decades. It wasn't anybody's fault. My colleague has a range of leadership skills and a pastor's heart. Members of the congregation believed passionately that what they were doing for or against the vision was "right." What is for sure is that it didn't turn out the way anyone intended. The saddest thing is the experience is not unique. It isn't even unusual.

So how does one navigate the complex journey of pastoring in the twenty-first century? How do pastors integrate these seemingly impossible (and, at times, incompatible) roles of master communicator, spiritual guide, organizational executive, program administrator, fiscal manager . . . all while conserving congregational values, expanding the financial resources, adding new members, and exploring the preferred missional future for a local congregation? Frankly, I don't know. And I don't know very many pastors who do.

What I do know is that twenty-first century pastors need *more* than the latest or best leadership and administrative practices infused with a dose of spirituality. I do know that they need *more* than an understanding of the importance of interpersonal skills (sometimes called emotional intelligence) injected with a dose of graciousness. I do know they need *more* than the latest effective communication tools for preaching or spiritual direction. I do know that they need *more* than a pithy organizational mission statement laced with biblical phrases or a strategic plan with measurable outcomes tied to descriptions of the Jerusalem church after Pentecost. Best leadership practices, strong interpersonal skills, effective communication tools and even focused mission statements and strategic plans are important and necessary components for pastoring. Good ministerial educational programs (formal and informal) should include them in their curricula. They are the building blocks of almost any kind of effective leadership in any organization. But these are not, in themselves, sufficient for twenty-first century pastors.

Pastors and church leaders in the twenty-first century need more than building blocks of effective organizational leadership. They need foundation stones that will allow their ministries to weather the storms of unreal expectations, theological controversies, competing agendas, conflicting values, and misinterpreted motives.

My own adventure of pursuing the "call to ministry" and pastoral and church leadership has spanned four decades in the varied contexts of the local church, a graduate seminary, and a Christian liberal arts university. I've experienced moments of spiritual and emotional heights that, at the time, seemed just short of the apostle Paul's third heaven experience of "paradise . . . [and] inexpressible things" (2 Cor. 12:4). I have also known moments of stress, disappointment, and failure as Paul describes in 2 Cor. 11 (i.e., the stresses of organizational leadership, the disappointments and failures of my own inadequacies and, occasionally, in those of others). Most of my life and ministry has been lived in the ordinary time in-between. Whether the moments are high, low, or ordinary I return often to the foundation stones to remember that which I have been called to be and to do.

STONE ONE: Servant Leadership in the Way of Jesus

First and foremost, I am called to be a servant, not a leader. The actions and responsibilities of leadership are inevitably part of the job description, but I must essentially lead from the heart and mind of a servant first—a predisposition to serving rather than leading.[1] This "servant first" way of leading keeps issues of power, authority, position, and ego in perspective. Leadership becomes stewardship rather than ownership. The church (or any other organization), the mission, the staff, the resources are not mine. As with my personal life and resources, it all belongs to God and I have the privilege of being a steward with the responsibility to maximize the potential of each. As one servant leader put it, "Stewardship involves partnership rather than patriarchy, and empowerment rather than dependency. This requires the deepening of one's commitment to service instead of self-interest."[2]

Servant leadership isn't a theory that will be replaced by the next fad to hit the popular book circuit. It isn't a style or method of leadership that one can use in particular situations when a "kinder" or "softer" approach may be more effective for the moment. It isn't one of several effective leadership practices from which one may choose. Servant leadership is a way of being and doing, in the way of Jesus; with the disposition of a servant's mind and the integrity of a servant's character, in the way of Jesus; in the servant actions in one's arenas of influence, in the way of Jesus. For the leader who is Christian, and particularly Wesleyan, there is no other way. Jesus reminded his disciples in the midst of their grumblings about greatness, "You know that the rulers of the Gentiles lord it over them, and their high officials exercise authority over them. Not so with you. Instead, whoever wants to become great among you must be your servant, and whoever wants to be first must be your slave—just as the Son of Man did not come to be served, but to serve, and give his life as a ransom for many" (Matt. 20:25-28).

In my last three offices, a simply crafted white pitcher, basin, and towel have been prominently displayed. These unmistakable symbols of Jesus, the Servant Leader, are not there for others to see, though on occasion I do have the privilege of sharing the foundation stone of servant leadership with others. The symbols are there to remind me that regardless of what office or position I may hold or regardless of whatever task may be mine for that day, I am a servant first—servant of Christ, servant of the gospel, servant of the church, and servant of the people I am to lead—that day and every day.

STONE TWO: Prevenient Grace

One of the occupational hazards of spiritual leadership is the tendency to perceive the results of ministry in terms of feast or famine. Worship, educational ministries, lay leadership development, community outreach, attendance, finances seem to be either going well (at times even extremely well) or they feel like ministry is stalled or completely stagnate. In the former, pastoral leaders are susceptible to the messiah complex where a sense of appreciation for one's able guidance can escalate into a sense of the absolute necessity of one's leadership. In the latter, they are susceptible to the sense of inadequacy and divine abandonment, sensing that God seems to be present and active everywhere else but where they are. Either situation can wreak havoc on one's sense of purpose and worth. I have experienced both more than once or twice.

The foundation stone of Wesley's understanding of prevenient grace keeps me from "thinking of myself more highly than I should," but it also keeps me from perceiving myself as being isolated in ministry with fading hope for the future. How does prevenient grace accomplish that?

Prevenient grace means that God is graciously and lovingly at work everywhere, all the time, with everyone and in everything. So wherever I serve, God is already there. I never walk into a worship service, a hospital room, a counseling session, a family conflict, or even a board meeting where God is not already present. Before every act of ministry I do, God's Spirit is already at work graciously drawing and wooing people toward God's will. Even if what I am doing doesn't seem to be working, God is. Words I utter "in his name" are spoken to hearers whose hearts and minds have already been prompted by the Spirit. Every sermon, every Bible study, every word of counsel whether brilliant, ordinary, or even substandard is still carried by the Spirit's wind. This is no excuse for laziness or mediocrity in ministry, but it is a comfort to know that my ultimate effectiveness is not solely dependent on me. This is, in part, what Jesus promised at the close of the Great Commission, "And surely I am with you always, to the very end of the age" (Matt. 28:20).

STONE THREE: The Promise of Transformation and the Hope of the Resurrection

Ministry is about the task of declaring and acting on the promise that in Christ all things can be made new. Paul's declaration in 2 Cor. 5:17, "Therefore, if anyone is in Christ, the new creation has come: The old has gone, the new is here!" (TNIV), is the great news of the gospel and is the heart of the message and motivation for every pastoral leader. What we are promising is not a self-help program of gradual improvement so that life is a little better, or at least a little more comfortable. We are not promising the transformation of one's employment or bank account. We are promising the transformation of the heart from one of stone to one of flesh. We are promising the transformation of the mind to one conformed to Christ rather than to the world. We are promising a change of perspective that sees life's situations through the eyes of a God whose love overcomes fear and whose grace overcomes selfish greed regardless of one's circumstances. If we surrender this promise of transformation, we have nothing uniquely Christian to say. Transformation is, of course, at the heart of Wesleyan theology and practice.

The ground of transformation is the hope of the resurrection. We declare in the Apostles' Creed that Jesus was "crucified, dead and buried . . . on the third day he rose again from the dead"—the first of everyone and everything that will be resurrected. We also declare our belief in "the resurrection of the body." We affirm that there is a complete resurrection coming in which the new heaven and the new earth of transformed material (i.e., "body") described in Rev. 21 will characterize our eternal existence with God, God's saints, and God's perfected creation.[3] Without this hope Paul reminds us that "our preaching is useless" (1 Cor. 15:14) and we are to be "pitied more than all others" (15:18, TNIV).

But the resurrection of Jesus was and is real, and we do have something to say. We join millions of pastoral leaders in witnessing the transformation of hearts and minds over two millennia of time. The new heaven and new earth are more than fodder for eschatological speculation. They are the hope of the future we declare in the gospel. When my limited intellect and vocabulary fails to provide adequate answers to life's dilemmas or perplexing enigmas, I am confident in declaring the good news that God's love and power expressed in the death and resurrection of Jesus is transformative and that our present circumstance, whatever it may be, is not what it shall one day be. The foundation stone of the promise of transformation and the hope of the resurrection means that I always have something to say in the present and a future reality to which I can point with anticipation. If any pastor can proclaim this, a pastor influenced by the optimism about grace found in the Wesleyan paradigm certainly can!

STONE FOUR: The Church as a "Sign" of the Kingdom

The church is not the kingdom. The church is defined by the saints past, present, and future. The kingdom is defined by the unlimited boundaries where God reigns, where God's will is accomplished. But though the church is not synonymous with the kingdom, it is connected to it by definition and purpose. The church is part of the kingdom as its primary advocate and its representative community. The church declares that, in Jesus, the kingdom has come and is coming. Similarly, the church bears witness to the reality and character of God's kingdom by being an incarnate community modeling what life in that kingdom looks like.

For centuries the church of Jesus Christ has struggled between the tension of being a living, organic community of relationships and being a structured institution with organizational charts, buildings, and budgets. Some have artificially divided these tensions into the spiritual work of ministry (i.e., the church as an organism) and the material work of ministry (i.e., the church as organization). This artificial separation sometimes extends to the absurdity of separating spiritual leadership (organism) and secular management (organization) or the real work of ministry from the necessary evil of administration. Seeing the church as organism and the church as organization, both with opportunities to be signs of the kingdom, helps me keep the rhythms of responsibilities in focus, whether they seem magnificent or mundane.

This fourth foundation stone helps me see each day and every task of pastoral leadership as another chance to guide a community of faith to be and act like a people engaged in God's mission and shaped by the character of Christ. In that kind of leadership there are no "necessary evils."

STONE FIVE: The Privilege of Partnership with God

Recently I was challenged to articulate a Wesleyan philosophy of Christian higher education. While I would never presume to have an exclusive description of that philosophy, I found the challenge most helpful in understanding the authentic purpose for the university where I was a servant leader and for the church under whose authority I serve. The Wesleyan affirmation of God's gracious intent to "seek and to save" and God's consistently loving acts of redemption, reconciliation, and restoration of all creation define the nature of Wesleyan education and pastoral leadership. To be called to ministry is to join with God in God's saving acts in the world. It is to find out what God is doing and join in the effort.

The essence of ministry in the Wesleyan tradition is not the defense of the faith, the denouncement of sin, or the pronouncement of judgment on evil people or things. The images of the Christian fortress from which we defend God's truth or the conquering Christian army taking back territory from the faithless infidels are not as compelling as joining the ministry of God's reconciling love as a foundation stone of pastoral leadership. God can defend himself. I'd rather be God's partner in redemption and love any day.

I have found these five foundation stones to be invaluable in my journey as a pastoral leader. Many of my pastoral friends have as well. Some have integrated them into their ministries in ways that God is honored and have been blessed with significant and meaningful growth inwardly and outwardly. But these stones won't guarantee a pastor will be a "success" in the eyes of the denomination or even clergy colleagues.

They won't provide job security in a pastoral assignment over the course of several years. Many who have lived and served by these principles have never pastored large congregations or been invited to join the "how-to" workshop circuit. Some whose ministries are characterized by these foundational stones have been "eaten up" by undue criticism or unreal expectations and have left ministry assignments (and the ministry itself for a time) under the clouds of interpersonal conflict and institutional stress.

So what is the sure outcome of a principle-based ministry built on the self-understanding of the pastor as servant of Christ, servant of the gospel, and servant of the church—i.e., the servant leader? The only guarantee is that when we come to the end of navigating this complex journey of pastoral ministry in the twenty-first century we can say with the apostle Paul, "Our conscience testifies that we have conducted ourselves in the world, and especially in our relations with you, with integrity and godly sincerity. We have done so, relying not on worldly wisdom but on God's grace" (2 Cor. 1:12, TNIV). Perhaps the greatest outcome is to come face-to-face with the Christ who called us and whose church we serve and hear him say, "Well done, good and faithful servant, let me help you with that towel and basin." That will be more than enough for me.

Discussion Questions

1. From your personal perspective, what are some other stress points of pastoral leadership in the twenty-first century that may be different from prior eras?

2. Are there models of servant leaders in your life? What are the qualities or actions they have that make them servants "in the way of Jesus"?

3. What might be considered spiritual about institutional administration when most of the management of material realities (e.g., boards, budgets, and buildings) are not that much different from other organizations?

4. How might other biblical images of the church (e.g., household of faith, body of Christ, kingdom of priests) inform pastoral theology and shape the practice of leadership?

5. Are there other foundational stones you have established in your own pastoral theology that have proved beneficial in times of challenge or disappointment?

Recommended Reading

Blanchard, Ken, and Phil Hodges. *Lead like Jesus: Lessons from the Greatest Leadership Role Model of All Times.* Nashville: Thomas Nelson, 2005.

Greenleaf, Robert K. *Seeker and Servant: Reflections on Religious Leadership.* San Francisco: Jossey-Bass Publishers, 1996.

_____. *Servant Leadership: A Journey into the Nature of Legitimate Power and Greatness.* New York: Paulist Press, 1977.

Smith, Fred, Sr. *Leading with Integrity: Competence with Christian Character.* Minneapolis: Bethany House Publishers, 1999.

Spears, Larry C., and Michele Lawrence. *Practicing Servant Leadership: Succeeding Through Trust, Bravery, and Forgiveness.* San Francisco: Jossey-Bass Publishers, 2004.

Tutu, Desmond. *No Future Without Forgiveness.* London: Rider, 1999.

Wright, N. T. *Surprised by Hope: Rethinking Heaven, the Resurrection, and the Mission of the Church.* New York: Harper Collins, 2008.

nine

"ORIENTEERING"
ADMINISTRATION AS WESLEYAN COOPERATION

~~

Stan Rodes

It was one of those phone calls that leaves you wondering (again) about why holy living seems to so frequently stub its toe in the week-to-week life of the church. The story was of a breach of trust and of testimony occurring in the inner workings of a community of believers bearing the Wesleyan label. The root of the problem, the caller declared, was "organized religion." This, of course, is an instance of profiling, if you will—a generalization based on guilt by association. The caller's conclusion suggests that organization is a blight upon every wing of the Christian church and that there's no particular way of administrating that lends itself to effectively partnering with God in his redemptive work in the world.

This judgment reflects a low view of the administrative dimension of the pastoral task—a view that can easily find a home even in the thoughts of those of us who would reject the caller's wholesale dismissal of "organized religion." By "low view" I mean the relegating of church administration to the category of "a necessary evil" at worst, and as a distraction to *real* ministry at best. It is a perspective that assigns most all of the theological weight of the Christian faith to the arenas of worship, preaching, and spiritual counsel, and reduces church administration to the ability to operate the church as a business. It is rare, for example, to speak of pastoral care and administration in the same breath—except, perhaps, as contrasting responsibilities. Not surprisingly, much of what is written on church administration zeroes in on helping pastors and lay leaders develop critical skill sets, primarily on the order of a business enterprise model. Without doubt, there is significant value in gaining such skill sets. However, to stop at this level is to settle for a low view of church administration and, in the end, to sell short our theological heritage as Wesleyans.

Rather than speaking to the "how to" of administration, I invite you to ponder with me the affirmation that there is a discernible Wesleyan paradigm that shapes the task of administrating the church—a paradigm that endures to the extent that it is thoughtfully and repeatedly contextualized rather than abandoned or reduced to a generic form of nonprofit, religious organizational management. This affirmation raises an intriguing question: *If there is a way of managing money and administrating the church that is identifiably Wesleyan, what are its distinguishing characteristics?*

I propose that there *is* an identifiably Wesleyan way of managing money and administrating the church. And I further propose that a truly Wesleyan understanding actually lends itself to a high view of church administration that, when properly apprehended and applied, results in administrating in a way that strengthens the life, ministry, and witness of the local church. To explore this conviction, it will be helpful to reconnect with the basic notion of administration in relation to the mission of the church.

"Orienteering": Catching the Drift

At the heart of most any complaint against "organized religion" is an indictment charging the church with having strayed from its true purpose and calling—of having become *dis*-oriented. This can happen easily enough.[1] Certainly, the reality is that unless a church is faithfully guided toward its purpose and calling it will drift toward disorientation. Administration is aimed at catching the drift and capturing a God-glorifying present and future. It is the pastoral[2] art of advancing vision, preserving commitments, nurturing relationships, and managing financial, material, and human resources for the sake of advancing the church in accomplishing its God-given mission.

While the idea of stewardship is essential to this pastoral art, the administrative act itself is best described by the root meaning of the word translated "guidance" or "gifts of administration" in 1 Cor. 12:28. The Greek word is *kybernetes* and means steersman, pilot, or helmsman.[3] Robert Dale makes a helpful observation about the responsibility and role of the helmsman: "In the same manner that pilots steer their ships through the rocks and shallows safely to their destinations, ministers guide their congregations toward their missions."[4]

This same imagery appears in Leonard Sweet's description of those communities of faith seeking to effectively navigate the high seas of the monumental changes taking place in our world. "AquaChurch" is the term he uses to describe those communities who understand that they are in uncharted territory and who are willing to forego maps (i.e., recipes, formulations, fill-in-the-blank charts) and forge ahead with an eye for signs and signposts. This requires the acquisition of a skill Sweet calls "orienteering."[5] While this skill is required of all communities of believers regardless of their theological stripe, what is distinctive about Wesleyan orienteering comes to light as we reflect on our theological heritage.

Orienteering and the Means of Grace

In 1744, John Wesley hand-selected a small group of leaders to confer together about developments in Methodist circles in what was still the early days of the historic Evangelical Revival. The questions considered at this first conference were not only doctrinal but also administrative. In addition to discussing what should be taught and how it should be taught, those attending the conference wrestled with "how to regulate our doctrine, discipline and practice."[6] In Wesley's view, answering only the first two questions without also providing a plan for conserving the burgeoning fruit of the revival was irresponsible and unacceptable. There was too much at stake. For the sake of both the saved and the seeking, the stability of each society was essential and required the regulation of doctrine, discipline, and practice.[7]

With this same concern in mind, James Anderson and Ezra Earl Jones recall us to the fact that "the activities of the church are not ends in themselves" but that "fellowship or worship or education or counseling are at their best means of grace."[8] This is a significant observation and reminds us that the idea of "means of grace"[9] belongs to the DNA of a Wesleyan understanding of the divine initiative in behalf of fallen humanity. And with respect to the subject of this chapter, one critically important outcome of conceiving of church administration itself as an avenue for the ministration of the means of grace is that it moves the center of gravity of administration from mere organizational efficiency or managerial effectiveness to an overt focus on saving the lost and discipling the found.

At the least, this means that a Wesleyan way of administrating the church is resistant to simply maintaining the status quo and insistent that every administrative endeavor be oriented to reaching a needy world. Although this is not peculiarly Wesleyan, to *be* Wesleyan *is* to share this core conviction. It may be helpful, therefore, to think of church administration as "ad-ministry"[10]—the practice of administrating from the conviction that administration is a critical contributive aspect of faithfully conveying the grace of God. Absent such a conviction, administration can actually become turned in upon itself— an outcome that is subversive of God's purposes and that, ultimately, plunders the morale and the spiritual vitality of the congregation.

True at the Core

In the day-to-day life of the church, managing money and administrating the church is where our theological convictions encounter real people who possess a mix of strengths, backgrounds, personalities, training, and idiosyncrasies. And it doesn't take long serving in a role of leadership before you realize that the community of the graced is not always gracious. We leaders frequently complain about this as we tell stories to each other of rankled members of the flock who give us headaches. But very often we do not see that we ourselves have had a sizable share in turning things a bit sour. Strangely, we seem puzzled by the fact that not everyone appreciates the whiplash effect of being blindsided by a decision that skipped the inconveniences of proper processes and procedures, or by our presuming that those who have given sacrificially already will gladly give more to cover the cost of the lack of thorough planning. Administrating the church in a Wesleyan way can actually help avert such scenarios, particularly if we are attentive to two concepts situated at the core of our theological heritage: cooperancy and connection.

Cooperancy

At the heart of a Wesleyan understanding of the cooperant nature of grace is the conviction that the grace of God is resistible and noncoercive—that it is extended to all, but foisted upon none; that it involves not only receptivity but response. How we translate this into "ad-ministry" is of critical importance. According to Alvin Lindgren and Norman Shawchuck, "Christ's Spirit is moving in the world, but the success of this commission depends on His best effort and ours. He told us the what, but depends on us to provide the how. . . . He leaves us at liberty to plan [it] and organize our work according to our best judgments."[11]

On the surface this appears as an affirmation of cooperancy. And, in a very basic sense, it is. However, it does not capture a Wesleyan

112

understanding of cooperancy. Taken at face value, Lindgren and Shaw-chuck's view contributes to a low view of administration: salvation is what God does, and administration is what we do. However, as Wesleyans we affirm that God neither leaves us out of the dynamics of his saving work nor does he leave us to our best judgments alone. It is not a matter of God's part and ours, but of "God with us." And in the daily life of the church as also in the individual's experience of God's saving activity, we are not sidelined by his sovereignty but are empowered by his Spirit "to will and to act according to his good purpose" (Phil. 2:13).

A Wesleyan way of administrating further recognizes that we together—both clergy and laity—labor with God in his redeeming work. The nature of this partnership is illustrated in a study of early Methodist missionaries by Carolyn Cordery in which she documents the Wesleyan resistance to viewing money as in tension with ministry (a "sacred-secular" dichotomy). She argues that these early Wesleyans regarded such a dichotomy as "at best, misleading, and at worst, inappropriate" and suggests that one of the keys to avoiding this polarity is to make certain that the laity do not feel excluded from sacred decision making in the church.[12] Sadly, this critical partnership in sacred decision making is too frequently trashed by a leader's drive to execute a personal vision by short-circuiting the greater time and effort involved in honoring commitments aimed at insuring that the leader and the community make the journey together.

Connection

A second concept standing at the core of our theological heritage is that of connection. In the Wesleyan framework, this connection is evidenced in three directions. First, we believe it is vital to retain connection with the *past*. This is not a defense for a "But we've never done it that way before" kind of response to new initiatives. Rather, it is a matter of seeing Christian tradition[13] as a critical resource of the church. A Wesleyan view considers it a grave error to administrate without sensitivity to the past or a sense of responsibility for the future. Faithfulness in managing the affairs of the church means there will be a conscious and conscientious contribution *in the present* that is amenable to the faith that was passed on to us and that forwards that faith into the future. Church administration in a Wesleyan way mandates that ministry resources and processes must be overseen by looking in *both* directions—to the past and to the future—in order to be truly faithful in the present. Whenever we orient our efforts with only the moment in view, our administration is shortsighted and ultimately self-centered and irresponsible.

Second, a Wesleyan paradigm values connection with each other as believers and with our neighbors, whoever they may be. A particularly good barometer of the value we place on this connection is our management of money. In this regard, John Wesley's admonition on the subject quickly comes to mind: "earn all you can, save all you can, and give all you can." To unpack its application to the administration of the church, it is important to consider its broader context: the Wesleyan commitment to good works as indispensable both to the life of faith and to the life together of the community of faith. This commitment is often summarized in Wesley's famous declaration, "The gospel of Christ knows of no religion, but social; no holiness but social holiness."[14]

When Wesley made this statement he was not speaking from the standpoint of the social gospel, so-called, that emerged in the early twentieth century. Though aspects of that emphasis would have resonated with him, he could scarcely have envisioned what Martin Marty has described as "Two party Protestantism": those who "focused on the saving of souls" and those who "focused on the sins of society, such as poverty and inequality, and asked people to seek salvation through building 'the Kingdom of God on this earth.'"[15] For Wesley, these two concerns went hand in glove.

However, when Wesley declared there is "no holiness but social holiness" he was standing his ground against those who called Christians to a life of seclusion "in order to purify the soul."[16] He himself contended for just the opposite: "It is only when we are knit together that we 'have nourishment from Him, and increase with the increase of God' . . . Solitary religion is not to be found [in the gospel of Christ]." Rather, "'Faith working by love' is the length and breadth and depth and height of Christian perfection."[17] Seeing relationship with others as vital to holiness is central to a Wesleyan way of managing money.

Consequently, in relation to money, a Wesleyan view rejects the notion of viewing money as the secular dimension of a sacred enterprise. On a very practical level, this means that the accounting of financial resources is perceived as sacred insofar as it genuinely services a stewardship mentality on the part of the church. Producing a report of income and expenses becomes a sacred endeavor when the accounting of past financial activity is compared with ministry objectives and commitments that reflect a prayerful discernment of the leading of the Holy Spirit at this point in time. It is this comparison and assessment that moves financial reporting *beyond accounting to accountability*. Such accountability informs the administrative tasks going forward: corrective measures are taken, development is paced and fine-tuned, and new ministry endeavors are launched.

While in principle most church leaders resist the secular-sacred distinction, a disturbing disconnect appears all too frequently in the administrative mind-set of local churches claiming to be Wesleyan. In these settings, pastoral leadership preaches principles of stewardship for the individual (urging faithfulness in tithing and sacrificial giving) while, as an organization, operating from the priority of attending to its own needs before giving to others. Thus, while individual members are called to "live by faith," leadership administrates "by sight." As a result, a stewardship mind-set is exchanged for a "proprietor" mind-set that is calculating and self-oriented.[18] Consequently, a schizophrenia emerges as the sacred is individualized while, at a corporate level, things operate in a secular fashion.

A Wesleyan view resists such schizophrenia. The financial management triad, "earn all you can, save all you can, give all you can," is aimed at pushing resources beyond ourselves. When Wesley spoke of saving he was not thinking in terms of putting money aside but of taking care to monitor expenses.[19] The aim was to truly love our neighbor as ourselves by making available all that we possibly *can* in order to relieve human need, beginning with those of the household of faith.

Third, in a Wesleyan paradigm, the notion of connection extends to the broader context of local churches in relationship with each other. While this sort of connectivity certainly has biblical precedence (2 Cor. 8), the imprint of the roots of Wesleyanism is particularly evident. John Wesley viewed Methodism as a renewal movement within his beloved Church of England[20] and gave clear instruction that Methodist preaching houses were *not* to be registered with the government as independent congregations. He also routinely urged his Methodists to attend church, and in doing so was *not* referring to their gathering in their societies; rather, he was speaking of their faithfulness to attend worship services of the Church of England each week.[21]

Connection, then, was not a matter of organizational efficiency or a franchising model designed to feed the bottom line of the mother organization. Remaining in connection was not simply an organizational model; it was an organizational *must*.[22] This is an important distinction and one that informs our understanding of the concept of connection as a primary element of a Wesleyan paradigm for administrating the church. It signals participation in a shared enterprise with purposeful coordination focused on a specific missional objective. This coordination was crafted to include *property*, *people*, and *doctrine* in an effort to assure both the continued alignment with that objective and the ongoing resourcing of that objective.[23]

A local church that operates in a Wesleyan way will perceive itself not as a congregation in loose affiliation with others of like persuasion but as integrally connected, and will value this connection through intentionally seeking to perpetuate the dynamic of connection as critical to the larger mission of the local church. When this is understood, there is a willing demonstration of support of shared purposes and a thoughtful engagement in furthering the good of the whole.

It would be misstating the facts to claim that the elements discussed above are *peculiar* to a Wesleyan understanding. And we certainly recognize that there are Christian leaders of other theological persuasions who are equally passionate about harnessing the church's resources to effectively reach a needy world. What *is* helpful is to grasp what is *identifiably* Wesleyan with respect to managing money and administrating the church, and to recognize the value of our theological heritage for our day-to-day leadership of those we serve.

Discussion Questions

1. In your own church setting, in what ways do current attitudes and/or practices reflect a low view or a high view of church administration?

2. What are some examples of how administrating might serve as a ministration of the means of grace?

3. How might the affirmation that "we are not sidelined by his sovereignty but are empowered by his Spirit" influence your approach to managing money and administrating the church?

4. In the managing of money, what might it mean for a church to live by faith and not by sight?

5. In what ways might a fresh consideration of cooperancy and connection as elements of our Wesleyan theological heritage impact administrative practices in your setting?

Recommended Reading

Anderson, James D., and Ezra Earl Jones. *The Management of Ministry: Building Leadership in a Changing World.* New York: Harper and Row, 1978.

Bonhoeffer, Dietrich. *Life Together.* Translated by John W. Doberstein. San Francisco: Harper and Row, 1954.

Dale, Robert D. "Managing Christian Institutions" in *Church Administration Handbook.* Edited by Bruce P. Powers. Nashville: Broadman Press, 1985, 11-31.

George, A. Raymond. "John Wesley: The Organizer" in *John Wesley: Contemporary Perspectives.* Edited by John Stacey. London: Epworth Press, 1988, 108-14.

Klopp, Henry. *The Ministry Playbook: Strategic Planning for Effective Churches.* Grand Rapids: Baker, 2002.

Lightbody, Margaret. "On Being a Financial Manager in a Church Organization: Understanding the Experience" in *Financial Accountability and Management* 19, no. 2 (May 2003): 117-38.

Means, James E. "The Purpose of Management" in *Leadership Handbook of Management and Administration.* Edited by James D. Berkley. Grand Rapids: Baker Books, 2007, 349-56.

Thomas, Edward A., Bruce L. Petersen, and Bob Whitesel, eds. *Foundations of Church Administration: Professional Tools for Church Leadership.* Kansas City: Beacon Hill Press of Kansas City, 2010.

Wesley, John. "Minutes of Several Conversations." Edited by Thomas Jackson. Vol. 8 of *The Works of the Rev. John Wesley, A.M.* London: Methodist Publishing House, 1831.

_____. "The Use of Money" in *Sermons II.* Edited by Albert C. Outler. Vol. 2 of *The Bicentennial Edition of the Works of John Wesley.* Nashville: Abingdon Press, 1976–.

ten

VIA SALUTIS
DISCIPLESHIP ON THE WESLEYAN JOURNEY

～

Rondy Smith

As I sit in my office pondering this writing assignment, I am staring at the wall decor that faces me and presents my daily mission. It is a beautiful 9' x 6' National Geographic map of the world. Stenciled across the top border in Old English script is the infamous quote by John Wesley: "The World Is My Parish." My decorating inspiration was fueled by the zealous heart-passion of a new pastor, trained in the Wesleyan tradition, aspiring to another Wesley quote: "Do all the good you can, in all the ways you can, to all the souls you can, in every place you can, at all the times you can, with all the zeal you can." It is a daunting daily accountability measure.

Wesley's pastoral theology is Great Commission and Great Commandment reflective. Therefore, it is perfectly well suited to drive the discipleship emphasis needed by all pastors of the church of Jesus Christ. Dallas Willard affirms and drives discipleship down to the grassroots level by suggesting that "spiritual formation in Christlikeness should be the exclusive primary goal of the local congregation."[1] That is a provocative challenge to pastors.

"Spiritual formation in Christlikeness" will be our simple definition of discipleship, since becoming Christ's disciple means not just following, but learning to be like him. For us as a Wesleyan tradition with a renewed interest in discipleship, the spiritual formation process is also the path to holiness. The goal of holiness is the same goal of discipleship: the restoration of human beings to the image of God. "And we, who with unveiled faces all reflect the Lord's glory, are being transformed into his likeness with ever-increasing glory, which comes from the Lord, who is the Spirit" (2 Cor. 3:18).

Formulating a Wesleyan Discipleship Strategy?

How might a pastor in the Wesleyan tradition formulate a biblical discipleship strategy? The answer to that question is critically important if we agree with the challenge posed above, *that discipleship should be the primary goal of the local congregation.* I believe our holiness theology in particular demands that we pay attention to discipleship and accountability structures, though we may not have always done this well and have perhaps lost Wesley's original vision.

That very idea was at the top of my prioritized agenda some ten years ago when I answered the call to vocational ministry and began my first (and current) assignment as associate pastor for community life at Hermitage Church of the Nazarene. As a former college professor and business practitioner in the area of human and organization development (HOD), my skill set and passion for "forming persons and organizations" would easily translate to the parallel church world of discipleship and congregational development.

More importantly, however, I was personally experiencing an unparalleled level of spiritual growth and satisfaction in my own journey as a disciple of Christ. I had a nearly unquenchable thirst for the Word of God and a new mission to proclaim that Word to a hurting world. I set out to create systems, structures, and environments that would cultivate this same desire in my fellow pilgrims and ensure their progress on the holiness path. But better than any organizational design I might craft is the hunger and thirst I hope to model and inspire. That realization is the most important lesson I have learned about pastoring and discipling.

My primary task as pastor is to simply live among the people as a fully committed Christ follower and urge them to do the same. It is the Eph. 4 lead-by-example model. "As a prisoner for the Lord, . . . [I must] live a life worthy of the calling [I] have received" (v. 1). The roots of Pietism in Wesleyanism pave the road to pastoral discipleship. There must be a solid conviction that my personal piety matters. My faith will bear the fruit of righteousness in my life. Only then can I lead others, disciple others. Only then can I "prepare God's people . . . so that the body of Christ may be built up until we all reach unity in the faith and in the knowledge of the Son of God and become mature, attaining to the whole measure of the fullness of Christ" (vv. 12-13).

My friend and mentor Dr. William Greathouse urged pastors, "take time to be holy, then preach and pastor out of the overflow."[2] That is some of the best advice I've ever received. He said the church desperately needs pastors who are reproducing Christ in their preaching and in their relations with their people. We only reproduce Christ when we have lived with him and his living Word. Obviously, Wesley's whole life and ministry was based on his vision of God found in Scripture. From John Wesley's own Preface to *Sermons on Several Occasions* (1746) we find similar advice:

> God himself has condescended to teach the way: For this very end he came from heaven. He hath written it down in a book. O give me that book! At any price, give me the book of God! I have it: Here is knowledge enough for me. Let me be homo unius libri. [A man of one book.] Here then I am, far from the busy ways of men. I sit down alone: Only God is here. In his presence I open, I read his book; for this end, to find the way to heaven. . . . And what I thus learn, that I teach.[3]

This lead-by-example model illustrates that discipleship is inherently incarnational, or embodied in flesh. It is a lifelong process that takes place in the context of community. Vibrant, contagious disciples of Christ mentor others into that same abundant life in Christ as they live together in authentic relationship. To be a discipler is to be a faith mentor. "Follow me as I follow Christ," says the apostle Paul. The process of making holy disciples is a spiritual endeavor requiring the ever-present help of the triune God and leaders willing to walk with, wrestle with, and cry with the people becoming holy. The totality of Wesleyan theology drives toward touching real lives with real love. We, and the "little Christs" we replicate, are the incarnational, dialogical curriculum for any effective discipleship "program," one conversation at a time.

Life Together

For Wesley, the church became the way we are "socialized" into the kingdom. Part of this socialization process happens organically as we spontaneously share how Christ has transformed us, but we must also be highly intentional. Wesley understood this dynamic and provided his converts with a disciplined program of spiritual formation in the context of fellowship with other Christians and focused pastoral care. He organized his congregation into cascading levels of accountability for spiritual growth: the society, the class, the band, and twin souls. The success of Wesley's design is best described by his contemporary revivalist/evangelist George Whitefield. "Brother Wesley acted wisely. The souls that were awakened under his ministry, he joined in class, and thus preserved the fruits of his labor. This I neglected, and my people are a rope of sand."[4]

The contemporary "small groups" movement is simply the evolutionary development of Wesley's wisdom. Most congregations today that are successfully reproducing Christlike disciples have adopted some form of small-group discipleship as a core strategy. My local church is no exception.

The context where I minister collectively issues a clear call to a life of community-based discipleship through our simplified mission: *Connect with a community following Christ . . . a place to belong, grow, and serve.* Our first concern is to connect everyone we know to Christ; that primary life-giving relationship. Our Christ-centered corporate worship is the main vehicle for accomplishing this through Word and sacrament, prayer and praise. Alongside participating in corporate worship, we believe every person in our faith community should find a "smaller" place to belong, grow, and serve in order to be more intimately assimilated into Christ's body, the church. This core strategy is expressed as "community life" and as community life pastor it is my responsibility to facilitate these connections. The key components of the community life strategy are expressed as *iBelong, iGrow,* and *iServe.* Whatever you might call them, the basic premises of each flow naturally out of Wesley's vision.

The first set of groups is called *iBelong,* which are groups for fellowship based on life experiences. Sometimes, people need to feel they belong before they can believe. The only way to cultivate true belonging in a large church is to develop relationships in small groups, but smaller groups also need such opportunities. There needs to be a wide bandwidth or multiple points for entry into "belonging." We have many different types of groups from affinity-based to task- or purpose-based. It doesn't matter if you first connect through a ball team, a bulk meal cooking group, Mom2Mom support group, art camp, songwriter's group, or homeschool consortium. What matters is that you begin "doing life" with God's people and learn that we are not so weird and out of touch as you imagined!

Our second set of groups is our *iGrow* opportunities. This is where our discipleship emphasis is explicit. Jesus invites us to "follow him." Discipleship means learning his ways; learning to be like him.

To paraphrase the words of *The Message,* in Matt. 11:27-30, Jesus says, "Line by line, I'll show the way to my Father to any who will come and learn from me." We offer many different learning opportunities for spiritual formation. Some are classroom and knowledge based, such as Sunday school and other Bible studies and equipping classes offered on weekdays and Sunday nights. Some are more intensely relational like our Starting Point Groups (for those just beginning the journey) and our One-to-One Discipleship program or our pairing of Spiritual Running Partners (Wesley's idea of "twin souls"). Some are more experiential like our Lydia Prayer Groups or our Apples of Gold mentoring groups or our Men's Fraternity. Our people are encouraged to engage in at least one ongoing learning opportunity outside of corporate worship. Jesus also gave us the mandate to make Christlike disciples in all nations. We provide additional discipleship training resources and opportunities to participate based on desired levels of engagement. Key questions posed constantly to our congregants: Who is discipling me? Who am I discipling?

Our *iServe* groups emphasize ministry and mission. Jesus said, "The Son of Man did not come to be served, but to serve" (Mark 10:45). His example in Scripture is clear. We are to be servants. To the early Wesleyans, service was as much a means of grace as prayer. The local church cannot function without every member finding his or her place on the team to serve the body (Paul's model in 1 Cor. 12). Then, we are to reach out and serve our community and our world in the name of Christ. We help our congregants find their ministry and mission by conducting individual discovery interviews. We listen to their story, quiz them about their current heartbeat, and then help them discern how God might have shaped them for ministry through particular gifts and graces. We host Mission and Ministry fairs to connect current needs with interested persons and to motivate. We organize service projects and mission trips, always providing handles for people to grasp on to.

This community-based assimilation and discipleship process demonstrates that we best teach people how to be Christ's disciples by intentionally moving them through the natural rhythms of healthy body life in Christ and engaging them in the myriad of spiritual disciplines that help us grow in grace. Research by Gallup's Global Practice Leader for Faith Communities, Albert L. Winseman, suggests that congregational engagement drives spiritual commitment, not vice versa as we tend to think.[5] The twelve measures on Gallup's Congregational Engagement Index survey look strangely like discipleship practices; they are all about relational connectivity and accountability.[6]

The Ultimate Goal

The dream goal for all disciples is to be fully alive like Christ! A good discipleship process moves people into the transformative stream of grace and holds them accountable for progressing up the helical spiral of Christlikeness from "one degree of glory to another" (2 Cor. 3:18, esv). My favorite metaphor for the discipleship journey is climbing a spiral staircase.

With Christ as the center pole holding all things together (Col. 1:17), we wrap our lives around his life and allow him to take us from where we are into fullness of life in him (Eph. 4:13).

This image also illustrates the Wesleyan idea of a continuum of full salvation: from the prevenient grace that awakens us, to the justifying grace that saves us, to the perfecting grace that sanctifies us, to the renewing grace that grows us, to the completing grace that glorifies us when we shall see Christ face-to-face and be like him (1 John 3:2; 1 Cor. 13:12; Phil. 3:20-21). This *via salutis* or "way of salvation" is the critical issue for Wesley.[7] This model is synergistic, optimistic, progressive—all Wesleyan ideas regarding participation in the divine life (2 Pet. 1:3-11). (Wesley's sermons "On Working Out Our Own Salvation" and "The Duty of Constant Communion.")

This dynamic between divine grace and human cooperation is the key to discipleship. Helping others to understand God's part and their part is critical for success on the journey. Without intentionality on our part, we either float along aimlessly or we stagnate at a particular rung on the staircase, never able to escape the gravitational pull of the natural life. Millard Reed says, "We need the supernatural help of Christ to fire that rocket booster and get us into the next orbit of the upward call."[8] The hope is "attaining to the whole measure of the fullness of Christ" (Eph. 4:13). We need to continue to call our people into the transformative stream of grace where Christ can take them from where they are into fullness of life in him. But we also need to instruct them in our Wesleyan view that they must cooperate with Christ, and teach them specific ways to do just that. At the heart of this is Wesleyan synergism.

The practices and disciplines of ministry that are necessary to create holy disciples in my pastoral care are a sacred privilege. First as pastors we must live an authentically Christian life. We cannot give away what we do not possess. We must be constantly basking in the light of his glory with unveiled face, so that we can reflect that glory to the world. We need to be the incarnational curriculum of holiness to our people, constantly reproducing Christ in my preaching, teaching, giving, and serving. We must demonstrate the radical optimism that knowing Christ transforms lives in the here and now.

Second, we must engage others in the dialogue and process of transformative grace. That means making available participation in all the means of grace. We must lead in worship that is Christ-centered and sacramental. We must facilitate Bible study that begets personal Bible study. We must lead in prayer that births prayer. We must cultivate a community of friends where we love and nurture one another in the faith. We must create structures whereby we learn to serve one another and the world. We must exemplify lifestyle evangelism and challenge others to follow suit. Overall, we must be like Jesus who called disciples and calls us to follow him so that we can lead others to see, love, and serve the loving, saving God.[9]

Discussion Questions

1. As pastors, what personal and corporate spiritual practices do you practice to grow in your relationship with Jesus Christ?

2. What are some distinct aspects of a Wesleyan approach to discipleship?

3. In what ways is your local congregation creating a context to develop Christlike disciples?

4. Since discipleship takes place in the context of community, what are some intentional practices to help Christians grow in Christlikeness?

5. Who is discipling you? Who are you discipling?

Recommended Reading

Blevins, Dean G., and Mark A. Maddix. *Discovering Discipleship: Dynamics of Christian Education*. Kansas City: Beacon Hill Press of Kansas City, 2010.

Foster, Charles. *Educating Congregations: The Future of Christian Education*. Nashville: Abingdon Press, 1994.

Henderson, D. Michael. *Making Disciples: One Conversation at a Time*. Kansas City: Beacon Hill Press of Kansas City, 2007.

Leclerc, Diane, and Mark A. Maddix. *Spiritual Formation: A Wesleyan Paradigm*. Kansas City: Beacon Hill Press of Kansas City, 2011.

Matthaei, Sondra. *Making Disciples: Faith Formation in the Wesleyan Tradition*. Nashville: Abingdon, 2005.

Mulholland, M. Robert, Jr. *Invitation to a Journey: A Road Map for Spiritual Formation.* Downers Grove, IL: InterVarsity, 1993.

Tracy, Wesley E., et al. *The Upward Call: Spiritual Formation and Holy Living.* Kansas City: Beacon Hill Press of Kansas City, 1993.

Willard, Dallas. *The Great Omission: Reclaiming Jesus' Essential Teaching on Discipleship.* San Francisco: HarperSanFrancisco, 2006.

_____. *Renovation of the Heart: Putting on the Character of Christ.* Colorado Springs, CO: NavPress, 2002.

eleven

REACHING THE LEAST OF THESE
HOSPITALITY AS THE HEART OF WESLEYAN IDENTITY

Nell Becker Sweeden

John Wesley's practice of hospitality was directly connected to the church's mission to carry the good news out into the world. His life, ministry, preaching, and teaching can be characterized by the type of hospitality that *goes out*. It may seem odd to describe Wesley's hospitality as going "out," when hospitality is often conceived as inviting the stranger "in." But the way the church practices hospitality, however, is uniquely tied to the mission of the church—a mission that embodies both "going out" and "inviting in."

As Wesley grew and matured in his understanding of God's calling, he found himself in a society (and a century!) full of much social change and many social challenges. There were areas of the country (and the world) that the church did not reach. Many people at home and abroad were suffering because they did not have the gospel and because they were poor. Wesley started teaching and preaching during this period in which at least half of the population of England, mostly the laboring classes, could be considered poor. Indeed, God opened Wesley's eyes to see the needs of those around him and those in far-off and distant places. His passion led him to step out of a traditional parish setting to preach in the open air and sent him into homes, prisons, schools, and orphanages where he welcomed the poor with the good news of Jesus Christ. He was *going out* into the world to offer Christ's hospitality.

Hospitality Practice

A Christian understanding of the practice of hospitality comes from the Judeo-Christian tradition and scripture and centers around welcoming the stranger or "alien." In practice, it often involves members of a community inviting an unknown person in need into a home or congregation. The community often demonstrates the depth of their welcome to the stranger through sharing a meal and providing care and material assistance where needed. For Christians, this hospitality is broadly recognized as a moral and ethical responsibility because it witnesses to the welcome of God in Jesus Christ. Traditionally, people have understood this practice to mean that they should invite the stranger *in* rather than calling the community to venture *out*.

The Hebrew Scriptures describe hospitality as an important practice arising out of Israel's heritage. In fact, God repeatedly instructs the Israelites to welcome the stranger and to remember the aliens and foreigners because God's people know all too well what it is like to be strangers. Leviticus 19:33-34 reads:

When an alien resides with you in your land, you shall not oppress the alien. The alien who resides with you shall be to you as the citizen among you; you shall love the alien as yourself, for you were aliens in the land of Egypt; I am the LORD your God. (NRSV)

These verses are a list of God's instructions and remembrances for the people of Israel. First, when strangers or foreigners reside on Israel's land, the people of God must treat them with equality and dignity. God's words also remind Israel of their own history as strangers and wanderers in foreign lands. This language would have conjured up memories of their ancestors' exile and slavery in Egypt and reminded Israel of their calling as the people of God. Such language of recollection is peppered throughout the Hebrew Scriptures, reminding the Israelites of their identity and of how God rescued and provided for them (Deut. 10:19). The language used here in the Hebrew Scriptures essentially calls Israel to love the alien as themselves, which is also the heart of one of the two greatest commands Jesus shares in the Synoptic Gospels (Matt. 22:37-38; Mark 12:29-31; Luke 10:27)—to love your neighbor as yourself.

Jesus' life and ministry reveal many acts of hospitality, in which sometimes he is the host and sometimes the guest. Many scholars note the importance of Jesus fluctuating between acting as guest and host. It unveils how hospitality does not simply go one direction but that it usually involves acts of both giving and receiving. Often a guest in the homes of sinners, Jesus also acts as the host—offering gifts, teaching, performing miracles, and so forth. As a guest at the wedding at Cana, Jesus transforms water into wine, providing this gift for the guests (John 2:1-12). And when he washes the feet of his disciples, he performs the role of the host even though he is a guest (13:1-17). Of course, Jesus' hosting the disciples at the Last Supper is a paramount example of hospitality, and one that the church continues to enact today. On the journey to Emmaus, it is not until Jesus gives thanks and breaks bread, becoming the host again, that his disciples see who he really is (Luke 24:31-32).

Throughout the centuries and today, the church also recalls and enacts Jesus' hospitality in the Lord's Supper in its continual celebration of Holy Communion. Eating together in Holy Communion is a central way the church anticipates the Lord's heavenly banquet and God's coming kingdom. Eating together in ordinary meals and inviting strangers to share in these meals also unfold new possibilities to encounter the grace of God through others in the body of Christ.

Matthew 25:36-42, often referred to as the sheep and the goats parable, highlights the importance of hospitable actions—offering food, cold water, and clothing as well as paying a visit to one another—and equates them with helping Jesus Christ himself. Many scholars consider this passage the model of Christian hospitality, not only because it emphasizes the moral obligation to welcome the stranger as Jesus Christ, but also because it opens up the Christian to recognize that in the encounter with the stranger, one is welcoming Christ.

Many themes in the Epistles echo the importance of showing hospitality to strangers. In fact, Heb. 13:2 notes how in offering hospitality, some have entertained angels without knowing it. In Rom. 15:7, Paul urges followers of Christ to welcome one another as Christ has welcomed them. Earlier in the letter, he had reminded believers that in holy living, they ought not to neglect to show hospitality (12:13). The Greek word for hospitality, *philoxenia*, not only means love of the guest or stranger but also delight in the guest-host relationship. This delight is fueled by the expectation that God or Christ or the Holy Spirit will play a role in every hospitable encounter and action.

Hospitality as Mission

As early Christian communities practiced the hospitality they learned in the life of Jesus, their faithfulness brought about new expressions and patterns of hospitality. Many of these hospitality-oriented actions were central to what the early Christians identified as their mission in the world.

Christine Pohl, in her seminal work *Making Room: Recovering Hospitality as a Christian Tradition* (1999), describes several key aspects of Christian life that show the centrality of hospitality to Christian practice. First, she notes how shared meals helped the early church overstep cultural boundaries and start incorporating Gentiles into communities that were following Christ. Early missionaries also depended on the hospitality shown to them when they traveled to spread the gospel. Additionally, the early church was born in households and hospitality was central to creating family-like ties among followers of

Christ. Seeking to break down traditional sociocultural barriers, these communities nurtured deep care and provision for one another across race, class, and gender so that they might be transformed into one family in Christ. As the early church grew, leaders were concerned that hospitality needed to be extended in a more organized fashion so no one would be neglected; they gave certain Christians the responsibility to make sure traveling Christians and people who were poor were welcomed and cared for consistently.

While one could identify many of the early church's expressions of hospitality with the practice of "welcoming in," there are many others one could identify with the Judeo-Christian scriptural practice of "welcoming out." For example, early missionaries received welcome from the people in the places they went but, at the same time, welcomed new believers into the body of Christ. Similarly, the early Christian communities offered an outward welcome in extending their household to offer the good news in sharing their way of life with others. Today, hospitality as "welcoming out" may similarly require the congregation to go out its church doors to offer the hospitality of Christ to others.

Wesley's Context and Ministries

Wesley shared a similar concern in discerning how to bring the gospel to those *out*side the walls of Anglican parishes. In 1739, John Wesley was challenged by George Whitefield to "extend the walls of the parish," so to speak, and to kindle Christian renewal through small groups in Bristol, England. Wesleyan historian Richard P. Heitzenrater notes how the involvement of Whitefield and the Wesley brothers in revival in the British Isles through itinerant "field preaching" became part of the larger worldwide movement, including the Evangelical Revival in England, German Pietism in the late seventeenth century, and the American Great Awakening of the early eighteenth century.[1]

John Wesley at first was adverse to the idea of field preaching, noting in his journal that his concern for decency and order in his own life had led him to presume that the saving of souls only occurred in the church. Though outdoor preaching was not illegal, it was not widely embraced and even was associated with "poor priests" and dissenters. Yet, at the same time, Wesley was passionate about renewal in the church through his system of Christian bands, made up of five to ten persons who gathered for accountability, spiritual nurturing, and holy living. Whitefield convinced him that Bristol was an area where many were "ripe for bands" and so Wesley went.

Heitzenrater notes, "Wesley's own text for Sunday, April 1, from the Sermon on the Mount, brought to his attention 'one pretty remarkable precedent of field preaching.' That afternoon, he saw Whitefield preach from 'a little mount' on Rose Green to about thirty thousand people! The following afternoon, he himself 'submitted to "be more vile" by preaching outdoors.'"[2] From this point forward, Wesley committed his life to field preaching. This preaching did not take place in fields as the name suggests, but rather in any open-air location, which for Wesley included such places as graveyards or in market squares. Presently surprised by the hundreds and thousands he recorded coming to hear his preaching, he began to sense that God was calling him beyond the normal parish boundaries and practices. Through this experience, he came to declare: "I look upon the world as my parish."

As Wesley's field preaching increased, his system of societies and bands grew as well. The bands met together voluntarily at least once a week for confession, prayer, and spiritual growth. Through the bands, Wesley persistently emphasized the nurturing of holy living as a natural outgrowth of God's free grace received in justification. Heitzenrater notes, "The point was to encourage faith working through love, that the love of God might be shed abroad in their hearts and lives."[3]

Wesley and Holy Living as Hospitality

In his teaching and preaching, Wesley continually sought to advance the wholeness of God's salvation for humanity. His bands, classes, and societies were an educational system that nurtured works of piety *and* works of mercy. Wesley tirelessly insisted that people respond to God's grace through good works. In his sermon "On Working Out Our Own Salvation" he instructs: "For, first, God works; therefore you *can* work. . . . Secondly, God works; therefore you *must* work."[4] Working toward the wholeness of God's salvation took on many shapes and forms for Wesley.

The good works that Wesley himself lived and relentlessly encouraged in the people called Methodist were often motivated by the hospitable actions summoned in Matt. 25:31-46: "For I was hungry and you gave me food, I was thirsty and you gave me something to drink, I was a stranger and you welcomed me, I was naked and you gave me clothing, I was sick and you took care of me, I was in prison and you visited me" (vv. 35-36, NRSV). While Wesley resourcefully set up a number of systems to facilitate Christians patterning their lives after "God's sheep" in Matt. 25, he was adamant that each individual must respond on his or her own to God's call to offer hospitality to others.

In his sermon "On Visiting the Sick," for example, Wesley outlines how *every* Christian, with *no* exceptions, must visit the sick.[5] He goes through a number of circumstances in which people justify that they need not visit someone who is sick (i.e., trying to send a doctor or provide money in their stead). Wesley, however, clearly resists these excuses. He details how a doctor may do good for bodily health but does not fulfill every Christian's duty to do good for the souls of others. Additionally, he writes that as a Christian if you do not go visit the sick yourself, "you lose a means of grace; you lose an excellent means of increasing your thankfulness to God, who saves you from this pain and sickness, and continues your health and strength; as well as of increasing your sympathy with the afflicted, your benevolence, and all social affections."[6]

135

He adds, "One great reason why the rich, in general, have so little sympathy for the poor, is, because they so seldom visit them."[7] In fact, Wesley names the hesitancy on the part of the rich as "voluntary ignorance" and parallels it with the priest's and Levite's hesitancy as they both pass by the injured man on the other side of the road in the account of the Good Samaritan in Luke 10:25-37.

Wesley facilitated ways for Christians to assist the poor through works of mercy—from establishing schools for children and adults, to creating home remedies, to admonishing people to visit the sick and imprisoned and gather donations and clothing for the poor, to small business loans and cooperatives. These contributed to deeper social transformation in society and embodied hospitality as they spurred Christians to *go out* into the world and serve others.

In Wesley's sermon "Upon Our Lord's Sermon on the Mount, VIII," written in 1748, he remarks,

> We "charge you to be rich in good works"; as you have much, to give plenteously. "Freely ye have received; freely give"; so as to lay up no treasure but in heaven. Be ye "ready to distribute" to everyone, according to his necessity. Disperse abroad; give to the poor; deal your bread to the hungry. Cover the naked with a garment; entertain the stranger; carry or send relief to them that are in prison. Heal the sick; not by miracle, but through the blessing of God upon your seasonable support. Let the blessing of him that was ready to perish, through pining want, come upon thee. Defend the oppressed, plead the cause of the fatherless, and make the widow's heart sing for joy.[8]

These movements of *going out* evidenced even in Wesley's own challenge to preach outside the walls of the church, would guide the Methodists for centuries to come. Many Methodists after Wesley extended and fleshed out his innovative ministry on behalf of the marginalized, poor, and vulnerable. Wesley wanted everyone to visit the sick and offer hospitality to the poor because he knew that these acts would transform Christians into faithful followers of Christ. Doing these works of mercy alongside works of piety would open their eyes and were, therefore, considered a means of grace.

The book of Acts was written in the spirit of *going out* in the name of Jesus. The early followers of Christ went out to show the way of Jesus and welcome others into this new life. Leviticus 19:34 speaks of a rich tradition of hospitality to the stranger, but this tradition is in fact inverted in the early mission ventures of Christ's disciples. The people of God of today, far from being settled in the land and providing hospitality to strangers, often may find that they are sojourners in the world. Yet even though they are sojourners, Christians are to provide hospitality to the world.

In this same spirit, people today who are shaped by John Wesley may find themselves offering hospitality most suitably as they *go out* into the world and creatively embody the gospel in new ways and in new contexts.

Discussion Questions

1. How do practices of hospitality fit within the mission of your local congregation? How do they fit with the mission of the church in the world?

2. In your surrounding geographical community, where do you find persons who are most vulnerable or marginalized?

3. How does hospitality fit within your congregation's outreach programs? Are there needs in the community that your congregation does not reach?

4. Discuss works of mercy and works of piety and how these relate to the wholeness of salvation for humanity. What do these

mean? How is the gospel manifest in word and deed by your local congregation?

5. Are there other ways in which your community might rethink of hospitality as "going out"?

Recommended Reading

Bretherton, Luke. *Hospitality as Holiness: Christian Witness Amid Moral Diversity.* Burlington, VT: Ashgate Publishing, 2006.

Heitzenrater, Richard P. *The Poor and the People Called Methodists.* Nashville: Kingswood Books, 2002.

——————. *Wesley and the People Called Methodists.* Nashville: Abingdon, 1995.

Jennings, Theodore W. *Good News to the Poor: John Wesley's Evangelical Economics.* Nashville: Abingdon, 1990.

Koenig, John. *New Testament Hospitality: Partnership with Strangers as Promise and Mission.* Minneapolis: Augsburg Fortress Press, 1985.

Marquardt, Manfred. *John Wesley's Social Ethics: Praxis and Principles.* Nashville: Abingdon Press, 1992.

Newman, Elizabeth. *Untamed Hospitality: Welcoming God and Other Strangers.* Grand Rapids: Eerdmans, 2007.

Oden, Amy. *And You Welcomed Me: A Sourcebook on Christian Hospitality and Early Christianity.* Nashville: Abingdon Press, 2001.

Outler, Albert C., and Richard P. Heitzenrater. *John Wesley's Sermons: An Anthology.* Nashville: Abingdon Press, 1987.

Pineda, Ana Maria. "Hospitality." In *Practicing Our Faith: A Way of Life for a Searching People.* Edited by Dorothy Bass. San Francisco: Jossey-Bass, 1997.

Pohl, Christine. *Making Room: Recovering Hospitality as a Christian Tradition.* Grand Rapids: Eerdmans, 1999.

twelve

THE DIVINE DANCE
EVANGELISM IN A WESLEYAN MATRIX

~◦

Dana Hicks

Earth's crammed with heaven,
And every common bush afire with God,
But only he who sees takes off his shoes;
The rest sit round it and pluck blackberries.
—Elizabeth Barrett Browning

In Robert Fulghum's book *It Was on Fire When I Lay Down on It,* he tells the story of traveling back to the U.S. from Hong Kong and waiting in the Hong Kong Airport for the long ride home. He sat down at the gate waiting area across from a young American girl who was also traveling back to the States. Suddenly, the young woman in faded blue jeans and an old T-Shirt began to cry. Fulghum tried to ignore it at first but her tears turned in to sobs. Finally, Fulghum couldn't ignore it any longer, so he asked her what was wrong. A couple handkerchiefs and a box of Kleenex later she finally got out the story—she had traveled to Asia and had a wonderful adventure. She wanted to stay longer but her money had run out and she had been waiting in the airport to fly home on standby for two days with little to eat. She just received the news that a seat was waiting for her on the next flight. But the problem was she had lost her ticket. The plane was boarding and she could not find her ticket. She had reached the point of despair wondering if she was going to die in that spot.

Fulghum frantically helped her look through her possessions but the ticket couldn't be found. His heart was breaking for her and the only thing he could think of doing was inviting her to get something to eat. After dinner he would talk to the powers that be and try to get her home. She accepted his kind offer of warm food. Fulghum writes:

You stood to go with us, turned around to pick up your belongings and SCREAMED. I thought you had been shot. But no . . . it was your *ticket*. You found your ticket. You had been *sitting* on it. For three hours.

Like a sinner saved from the jaws of hell, you laughed and cried and hugged us all and were suddenly gone. Off to catch a plane for home and what next. Leaving most of the passenger lounge deliriously limp from being part of your drama.

I've told the story countless times. "She was sitting on her own ticket," I conclude, and the listeners always laugh in painful self-recognition.[1]

There are many aspects to Wesleyan theology that add value to the way in which we view evangelism but probably none bigger than Wesley's doctrine of prevenient grace. And like this ticket, it is closer than we know. Prevenient grace is simply the grace that precedes salvation. Wesley himself described it as "the first wish to please God, the first dawn of light concerning his will, and the first slight transient conviction of having sinned against him."[2]

But even before salvation, before we repent of our sins and accept Jesus as Savior, prevenient grace is a recognition that although we humans have been corrupted by the effects of sin, the image of God remains in us to the extent that we are not totally corrupt or twisted. Every one of us, no matter how broken, lives in a God-soaked universe in which God is at work in everyone's life, drawing them to himself. To borrow Robert Fulghum's image, we are sitting on our tickets—oblivious to how close we are to our Creator; painfully unaware of how close we are to salvation.

Wesley's thought stands in sharp contrast to our friends in the Reformed tradition in which the idea of total depravity rules the day. Our Reformed friends believe that because of the fall of humanity, people are enslaved to sin and estranged from God to the extent that we are deserving of nothing more than his wrath, often concluding that our only hope is God's predestination.

But for those of us in the Wesleyan tradition, we find grace in unexpected places. Often recognizing God's grace and presence in the world is akin to an exercise in art appreciation. It takes training and it takes experience, but we can begin to recognize the fine nuances of God's handiwork in places in which we might least expect it. We begin to find his fingerprints all over people that we may have written off. I like the way one author describes evangelism:

> [Evangelism] is less about the transportation of God from one place to another and more about the identification of a God who is already there. It is almost as if being a good missionary means having really good eyesight. Or maybe it means teaching people to use their eyes to see things that have always been there; they just don't realize it. You see God where others don't. And then you point him out. So the issue isn't so much taking Jesus to people who don't have him, but going to a place and pointing out to the people the creative, life-giving God who is already present in their midst.[3]

Wesley seemed to understand that effective evangelism begins with accurate theology—a good understanding of the nature of God. Part of Wesley's theological influence came from the Eastern Orthodox tradition.[4] Unlike the Western church that we in the U.S. have been informed by, the Eastern church described God in much more relational terms. "God is love," the Bible declares (1 John 4:16). Orthodox theologians concluded that the love of God must exist as an eternal movement among the members of the Trinity, or *perichoresis*. *Perichoresis* can be literally translated as "dancing." In effect, the love of the Trinity is the holy dance of God, a living out of the loving relationships among Father, Son, and Spirit. The holy dance exists because God is love.

Recent understanding of the nature of quantum particles suggests that the structure of the universe also appears to be based on relationships. Quantum particles do not really exist in isolation; rather, they exist in relationship to each other. Researchers have only scratched the surface of the complex relationships between matter, energy, space, and time. At the Center for Non-Linear Studies in Santa Fe, New Mexico, matter is speculated to be nothing more than vibrating threads of energy. Human bodies are the organization of "dancing energy."[5] Every atom of creation is putting off a vibration, much like sound or a dance.

The beginning of the Bible is a hymn, a creation hymn of how God created the world: "And God said, 'Let there be light,' and there was light" (Gen. 1:3). Creation was sounded forth, literally. Sound became sight. Cosmic vibrations became galactic visions.[6] In short, the "glue" that holds the most basic building blocks of the universe is literally a dance that takes place interrelated to one another similar to the Trinity's dance.

God's activity in continually creating his universe is also the product of vibrations. Sound waves may have helped shape how the cosmos was structured by organizing the pattern of galaxy clusters and voids seen in the night sky. Alexander S. Szalay argues that the acoustic oscillations (matter in motion), given off when the universe was a cosmic soup and fog of protons and electrons, helped to structure the matter of the universe into galaxies and galaxy clusters.[7] He and other scientists argue that the world is the creation of acoustic waves or, in effect, matter in motion.

Consequently, the God of the holy dance relates not just to himself but also to the world he has created. As one resonates with the holy dance, one is resonating with the created order of the universe. Since the creation of the world, our Trinitarian God has been constantly reaching out with love to humanity. As a result, evangelism does not begin with Matthew's Great Commission to "go and make disciples"; rather, it begins in the heart of God, at the core of his being. Jesus speaks to his disciples in John 20:21-22: "Again Jesus said, 'Peace be with you! As the Father has sent me, I am sending you.' And with that he breathed on them and said, 'Receive the Holy Spirit.'" Evangelism is from God, through the Son, in the power of the Holy Spirit. It is not fruit of a divine strategy meeting but simply a reflection of who the Trinity is and is experienced at the heart of creation.

Yet, love, by its nature, does not stay inward-focused but becomes other-centered. The core of God's being is to go outside of himself. The salvation history of God reflects the continual reaching of God out from himself: creation *ex nihilo,* the redemption of the world by Christ, and the ultimate consummation of history as the Spirit draws all of creation to his love. All of these acts outside of the Trinity are a reflection of the love inside the members of the Trinity.

Therefore, an accurate understanding of God as loving and triune enables one to see God not as a ball of energy or some kind of force but in very personal terms. An accurate understanding of the Trinity helps one see God as One who will stop at nothing to reach humanity.

As followers of God, especially as pastors, our evangelism is patterned after this love and, on a deeper level, participates in God's love. Evangelism, in its purest form, flows out of one's relationship with the Trinity. When one repents, receives God's acceptance through Christ, and experiences the Spirit's assurance of being God's child, one's life is caught up in the inner love of the Trinity. As this happens, one is also caught up in this other-centered love for humanity. One is caught up in the dance of the Trinity. Jesus illustrates being caught up in the inner love of the Trinity in his prayer to the Father that says, "I have made you known to them, and will continue to make you known in order that the love you have for me may be in them and that I myself may be in them" (John 17:26).

When two vibrating energies move toward each other and those vibrations are in sympathy with each other, it is called "resonance" in the world of physics. One has an intuitive sense of resonance in the common vernacular. When two people resonate, one says that they are "on the same wavelength" or "in tune with each other." Enormous energy is released in resonance. Physically speaking, when the frequency or vibrations of one entity matches the frequency of another, a tremendous explosion of energy ensues. The explosion of energy has happened in places like the Tacoma Narrows Bridge in Washington. When the wind passing through the Puget Sound created a double oscillation that matched the frequency of the bridge, the bridge collapsed. Clemson University officials discovered something similar. After an investigation as to why their stadium was crumbling, they discovered that the song "Louie Louie" gave off frequencies that perfectly matched the frequency of the stadium.[8]

When one is in tune with the resonance of the Trinity, spiritually speaking, enormous energy is also released. One becomes a conduit of the love of the Trinity for the world. This is prevenient grace—resonating with a love that is at the heart of God's creation—even when we are completely unaware of it. This model of prevenient grace understands that the pastor's role in reaching people transcends the methods we use to "get people saved."

The power of the truth of prevenient grace was driven home to me at my ten-year high school reunion. When I returned to the town in Oregon that I grew up in, I was able to reconnect with old friends, many of whom didn't know what to do with a pastor in their midst. So, in an attempt to avoid awkward conversations, many of my friends kept referring me to a fellow classmate—Ellen. "You should talk to Ellen. She's really religious now," they told me.

Ellen and I were not close friends in high school. Ellen was a very bright adolescent, but we ran in different circles. Ellen was part of the punk rock scene of the 1980s and was considered liberal in every sense of the word even in a liberal state like Oregon. She was not just anti-institutional but an anarchist. Not just anti-Christian but bordering on atheist. Frankly, I would have been less surprised if they said that Ellen turned in to a unicorn; but instead Ellen had "got religious."

When I tracked down Ellen, a lot had changed in her life. She recounted to me how after high school she had been accepted at Reed College in Portland (the same Reed College that Donald Miller spoke of in *Blue like Jazz*). She majored in agricultural science with the hope that she could drop out of society and live a self-sustaining life in the Oregon wilderness. She partied a lot, did a lot of drugs, and began dating. Her life was going just the way she expected until she got pregnant as a college sophomore. Ellen told her boyfriend that she was not going to abort the baby. So he insisted that he was going to help her raise the baby. And in a move that may have surprised even God, he proposed to her and they got married.

The honeymoon quickly ended when the realization hit them that now he was a college dropout with a young wife and baby on the way and no marketable skills to get work. So he did what every anarchist liberal does when things go poorly—he joined the army. And in an irony worthy of O. Henry, he was stationed with his young wife to Fort Hood, Texas. Ellen said that for an anarchist liberal from Oregon, this was like moving to the moon. She knew nobody, and the military culture was very different from what she was used to. But Texas was the biggest shock of all—moving from the most unchurched state in the United States, from the campus of Reed College, to what is in many ways the buckle of the Bible Belt, was unnerving to both of them.

Ellen began spiraling into depression and isolating herself on the military base housing. Her next-door neighbor began making efforts to reach out to Ellen and in spite of their many differences they became friends. Ellen said that in spite of the fact that her neighbor was a Christian, she really liked her. The only drawback to their friendship was that the neighbor kept inviting her to church—almost weekly. Finally, Ellen agreed to give the church a try so that her neighbor would get off her back.

Ellen was nervous the Sunday she first entered the church. She had only been inside a church one other time in her life—for a family wedding—and was unsure what to expect. She told me that as the service began, the band began to play worship music. The congregation stood and she listened very closely to the words the people were singing. She recounts:

> Then the most amazing experience of my life happened. There was this . . . Presence that came over me. It was in some ways like nothing I had ever experienced but in many ways, it was a Presence that I had known my entire life. I was so overwhelmed that I literally fell to my knees right there and began to cry. Then I began to sob. The band played on and my friend wasn't sure what to do. I cried through the entire music set. I cried through the pastor's sermon and never really heard much of what he was saying. When the service ended, a pastor from the church asked me, "Would you like to pray?" I said, "I think so." And that is how I gave my life to God.

These days Ellen serves at a church in Washington State as a director for worship arts and drama. But the lesson I learned from Ellen is that God is at work through his prevenient grace in the lives of people that I might think are far from him. He is at work in places where I would never imagine him showing up. My job as a pastor-evangelist in the Wesleyan tradition is to find those points of contact where God is already at work in a person's life: hear the music, resonate with the music, and learn to dance with the sound and movement of the Trinity. One important author uses the metaphor well:

> Evangelism as dance begins with something beyond yourself. Think of a song that comes to you. . . . At first you may catch only a note here, a phrase there, and it may sound strange. But once you really *hear* it, . . . once it finds its way into your soul and begins to play there, it feels so familiar . . . that you wonder if you have made it up yourself. Yet the song's splendor . . . convince[s] you that its origin lies beyond your own imagination. . . . You find yourself humming the song, tapping your finger to it, whistling it, . . . and you wonder "Where did this come from? Who wrote this song? How did it get into my head?"
>
> So the gospel comes to you not like a commercial on . . . TV or a political slogan in a campaign or a scientific formula in a classroom, but like a song. It sneaks up on you, and then sneaks inside you. Somewhere in your journey through life, you begin to hear this song whose music captures your heart with its rhythm, melody, ambience, and glory, and you begin to move to its rhythm. Thus you enter the dance.
>
> Over time, your whole life begins to harmonize to the song. Its rhythm awakens you; its tempo moves you, so you resonate with its tone and flow with this melody. The lyric gradually convinces you that the entire world was meant to share in this song with its message, its joy, its dance. [original emphasis][9]

Pastors, invite others into this marvelous dance. This is the real meaning of evangelism.

Discussion Questions

1. Have you ever had the experience of "sitting on your ticket"— of discovering God in a very close and unexpected place?

2. Is there someone in your circle of influence right now who seems to be very far from God? If so, who is it?

3. How are art appreciation and evangelism in the Wesleyan tradition similar? What are some ways that you can learn to appreciate the image of God in other people?

4. What are some ways that a person can learn to hear, resonate, and dance with the music of the Trinity?

Recommended Reading

Clapp, Rodney. *A Peculiar People: The Church as Culture in a Post-Christian Society.* Downers Grove, IL: InterVarsity, 1996.

Crandall, Ron. *The Contagious Witness.* Nashville: Abingdon, 1999.

Guder, Darrell L., et al. *Missional Church: A Vision for the Sending Church in North America.* Grand Rapids: Eerdmans, 1998.

Hybels, Bill. *Just Walk Across the Room.* Grand Rapids: Zondervan, 2006.

Hybels, Bill, and Mark Mittelberg. *Becoming a Contagious Christian.* Grand Rapids: Zondervan, 1994.

McLaren, Brian D. *More Ready than You Realize: Evangelism as a Dance in the Postmodern Matrix.* Grand Rapids: Zondervan, 2002.

Moltmann, Jurgen. *The Trinity and the Kingdom.* San Francisco: Harper and Row, 1980.

thirteen

GRACEFUL INCLUSION
SPECIAL NEEDS AS A TEST OF WESLEYAN ECCLESIOLOGY

~⌒

Joy Wisehart

One day my son Brady, a pastor in Tulsa, was having lunch with some friends at Cracker Barrel. As their orders were placed on the table, he turned to the waiter and said, "My friends and I are going to pray before we eat; is there anything we could pray about for you?" The waiter paused, taking that in and replied, "Yes, would you pray for my son?" When Brady inquired about his son, the waiter pulled out a picture of a young boy and said, "Yes, please pray for him. He struggles with autism."

Brady told him that he was a pastor and invited his son and him to come to Family Church. "We're not sure what all we need to do to minister to you and your son, but we would sure like you to come. We promise we would love you." The waiter's face lit up. He paused and said, "I've been looking for a place that would love and accept us as we are." The waiter walked away from the table with tears in his eyes.

Sarah had contacted the church around the corner when her son Ben turned three years old. She felt like her family needed to get into church. Her son's seizure disorders had kept her close to home, but now she felt Ben needed social contact with other children. Sarah was amazed to discover the church wouldn't allow Ben to be in Sunday school at all. Another church she called said they could come but he would have to stay in the baby nursery.

Toby was an active six-year-old with autism. About midway through the Sunday school hour, his parents were contacted and told to come get him—the adult workers just couldn't handle his behavior. They were asked to find another church stating, "We just can't meet his needs."

Jennifer had sensory issues. Imagine how her mom felt when she was told her two-year-old daughter was "a little spoiled" and maybe she was acting out in church just to get attention.

Dick and Thelma had been thinking about attending church for some time. They were not regular attendees but wanted to break that habit and start going to church. Their son, John, had been with them for thirty-two years, had heart trouble, and was now bound to a wheel-chair, no longer able to walk because of severe rheumatoid arthritis. They felt excited about the beginning of this new resolve. They were quickly disappointed when they arrived at church to find that after getting through the front doors, no other doors were wide enough to receive John's wheelchair. After several tries, they gave up, went home, and decided attending church was too hard, and they never darkened a church door again.

When families with children or adults who have physical, emo-tional, or mental needs visit churches, they are too often met with "We can't meet your needs here" or "We just can't help you" and they never return to that church or, often, to church anywhere. Children with disabilities often find the church doesn't welcome or truly value them. There really isn't a place for them when children scamper off to Sun-day school or children's church on Sunday morning. And the children aren't the only ones who suffer. The challenges of dealing with family members in the home with special needs are overwhelming, and many families face those challenges without the church's intentional, active involvement.

Many children with disabilities feel spiritually and socially isolated. The law mandates their inclusion in the public school classroom, but we don't see that same percentage in church programs for children. We don't see that inclusion in church parties and teen sleepovers either.

Our daughter, Amy, was diagnosed with Asperger's syndrome in her later teen years. At the church we were pastoring, she longed to feel some sense of inclusion and hospitality from the church as a whole, but specifically from her age mates. Too often she watched as parties were planned, sleepovers were arranged, and she was not included. She would stand there in the group of her peers as they walked away laughing, enjoying one another, looking forward to their fun, and no one had invited her. Her heart was broken. As parents, our hearts were broken. When we include these special children in a small-group community, like Sunday school and Sunday school events, we minister deeply to that child's heart as well as to the entire family.

In her book *Copious Hosting: A Theology of Access for People with Disabilities* Jennie Weiss Block suggests that of all places, the church needs to be the model of accessibility, the point of entry into God's love that is shown by her action and thinking. The body of Christ presumes a place for everyone. But place is difficult for people with special needs, for far too often people with difficulties encounter a symbolic sign that says "access denied." The goal should be warm, loving communities of abundant hospitality, a fruitful metaphor for divine love.[1] Thomas Reynolds's book *Vulnerable Communion: A Theology of Disability and Hospitality* implies hospitality means actively, warmly befriending the stranger, not as a spectacle, but as someone with value, created in the image of God and having unique gifts to offer as a human being.[2] Block suggests,

At the heart of the Christian witness is an inclusive love of difference that is christological in shape. In the Christ event, God sympathetically enters into our midst and communicates a love that spills over with unconditional regard for all persons. Beyond merely confirming the basic human right to respect, this radical love issues recognition and acceptance of humankind as a bearer of the image of God. And it does so in a gesture of hospitality.[3]

My friend Michelle Mosier is a pastor in Ohio. She and her husband have two sons, both with autism. Mitchel, her twelve-year-old son, wanted to go to church camp. Michelle made the decision to allow him to go and she would accompany him as her son's "buddy." At dinner the first night, the person in charge called on her son to pray for the meal. He gladly agreed to pray, but because of his disability, and the group being unfamiliar with him, no one could understand his speech. When Michelle's son was done praying, the person in charge called on someone else to pray—a person whose language all could understand. In this experience, this young boy was not validated nor was that camp an experience of hospitality, accessibility, warmth, and a celebration of one created in the image of God. Who is to say that the Lord did not hear his prayer or that the campers needed a more able someone to pray whose words were more articulate?

In the book *Special Needs, Special Ministry for Children's Ministry* the National Organization on Disability declares there are fifty-four million people in the United States with disabilities.[4] One in five Americans has some sort of disability. What percentages are in our church? Are we addressing these needs? Have we even thought about this slice of our culture? Is this population missing in our church? Do we say in so many words, "Let the church down the street minister to those individuals"? Do our actions imply, "Really, we are not called to minister to special needs people"?

Our love of God and his people informs us how the church might accommodate those with disabilities and special needs. What would ministry to special needs children and adults do for churches that choose to be inclusive and love them? For starters, the church would be fulfilling the *Great Commission* in Matt. 28:16-20. A person with a disability is first a person who needs to be redeemed and nurtured. Everyone everywhere should be invited to hear and respond to the gospel. Is there somewhere in Jesus' command that the gospel should be shared with just the able-bodied or those with no physical, emotional, or mental disability?

Jesus gave advice to those planning a party and said, whoever you invite, be intentional about including those with special needs. According to Luke 14:13-14 where he admonished, "But when you give a banquet, invite the poor, the crippled, the lame, the blind, and *you will be blessed*" (emphasis added). Inclusion of special needs children and adults will give a two-sided blessing—it will bless those included and bless the church and its members.

Jesus was on his way to Jerusalem for a feast of the Jews in John 5:1-9, "Some time later, Jesus went up to Jerusalem for a feast of the Jews . . . here a great number of disabled people used to lie—the blind, the lame, the paralyzed" (vv. 1, 3). There near the pool of Bethesda was a man who had been crippled for thirty-eight years. Even though Jesus was on the way to another place, his heart was touched for the less abled, the weak, and the individuals with special needs. So he stopped, ministered, touched, and healed the "invalid" by the pool. Do we validate who the world invalidates?

Abandoning ourselves to care for another always seems more attractive as an abstract ideal rather than a concrete reality. Once we encounter another person's difference from us, we are giving up our hold on reality as we see it and letting something "different" into our own space. Letting go and loving and becoming open to another in love is an experience of, as John Wesley says, "the love which our Lord requires in all his followers, the love of God and man." This love is spoken of in Rom. 5:5, "God has poured out his love into our hearts." What does God ask of us, ask his church to do? Really the answer is simple—it is just to love. Do our holiness churches show the love of God to *all* that come in the doors? Do we show the love of God by reaching out and intentionally including those with differences from us, emptying ourselves to care for another as our reality? In doing so it gives power to the deepest kind of mutual belonging imaginable, transforming us in the direction of the divine itself.

Josiah lives in Ohio. He wanted desperately to go to church camp. Both his parents worked and had other children in the home. He had special allergies and a strict medical regimen. A policeman in the church heard about Josiah and felt the Lord tugging at his heart and took a week's vacation to go to camp with him. He was his special buddy all that week. How do we live holy and human? That policeman had found the answer.

I am convinced by the words of Nancy L. Eiesland that "ignoring disability means ignoring life." For the grouping "of our lives into categorizations of good and bad, pain and pleasure, denies that the lives of people with disabilities, like all ordinary lives, are shot through with unexpected grace."[5]

My husband and I are blessed with two wonderful children, both with disabilities. Our son grew up struggling with severe asthma, which twice almost took his life. As mentioned earlier, Amy was diagnosed with Asperger's syndrome. Both of these children have given us such great joy and even though there were many painful times, we are thankful not to have missed the "unexpected grace." When can grace be seen? Could it be that grace can be seen "when pain is allowed to be pain, weakness is allowed to be weakness, and our thorns are not explained away?"[6]—especially in the church.

There is a striking picture in Matt. 19:14: "'Let the little children come to me, . . . for the kingdom of heaven belongs to such as these.' When he had placed his hands on them, he went on from there." There is nothing he did or said anywhere in his ministry that proposed children couldn't be on crutches, in wheelchairs, or developmentally disabled. He loved and welcomed them all. One of the conclusions I have come to is that everyone in our lives is a "gift" from the Lord; each one is wrapped differently.

Is there a biblical, theological basis for ministry to children and adults of special needs? I believe the Word of God speaks to this by suggesting the following:

All people are created in the image of God. Genesis 1:26 says, "Then God said, 'Let us make man [male and female] in our image, in our likeness.'" His image is uniquely reflected in all people—this is not just for the "abled." God's image is sometimes revealed in twenty perfect, little fingers and toes. At other times, it's seen in tiny, twisted limbs and bright, crooked smiles. Babies born with physical limitations aren't a mistake of nature—they're a new means of grace. They are no less created in God's image if they have mental, emotional, or social limitations either.

All people have special gifts. First Corinthians 12:4, 6: "There are different kinds of gifts . . . but the same God works all of them in all." We all have certain gifts to compliment the body of Christ. Is there one gift that is not needed? Which one can we do without? No one is unnecessary. But even more, Paul states that those parts that may seem "unpresentable" are given special honor! Churches that include those with disabilities often have the wonderful experience of seeing how God can use such persons in incredible ways. Paul's metaphor in this passage also reminds us that we aren't just helping those who seem needy; we also *need* them! God envisions a truly interdependent body where all are valued, all are contributors, and all are needed.

The church is meant to turn the world's value system upside down. If we don't have those with special needs in our church, the church is lacking! We should always remember that those with "special needs" should also be called those with "special gifts." All are invited into the kingdom of God and empowered to benefit the body of Christ, the church and the community.

This chapter has not been written as a how-to chapter but has been written to cause the reader to evaluate the implications of the holy life and think how the life of holiness would love and minister to all— the able and the dis-abled. As a pastor of or in your congregation, give consideration to the following when thinking of your place of ministry. Will your church welcome those adults and children with special needs and ultimately lead them to salvation, and nurture them throughout their lives?

You may be asking, how do I begin?

- **Pray**—Begin here by praying for the ministry, its leaders and those to whom you will be ministering. How will you reach out in the community? Are there people in the church that share this passion? Do we have any families with special needs that already attend the church?

- **Prepare**—What is needed to get ready for this ministry? What is the special needs culture in the community where you live? Prepare for a mind-set that is inclusive, warm, accessible, and hospitable. Consider the changes that may be needed to receive new people into your Sunday school and church services. Of course parents of special needs children will have a passion, but they cannot always run this ministry. They need a break from the continual care of their family member. Begin slow, "one child at a time." Offer a one-night-a-month respite for the families. I know one church that had "buddy soccer." Each child that played had a buddy playing alongside him or her, and even though they enjoyed the fun of scoring, there was no winning team—just fun playing the sport. The thrill of it was evident on the faces of these children.

- **Plan**—Educate yourself and your church. Walk around your building and the parking lot. Check ramps, restrooms, doorways, handrails, and so forth—all meeting the designated requirements. Is your church building assessable to all? Promoting this ministry from the pulpit is much more effective than a bulletin, and it shows your support. Bathe all this in prayer seeking the Spirit's leadership.

Nothing speaks to the point of this chapter as an illustration taken from the life of Kathleen Deyer Bolduc titled "For Me!" from her book *Autism and Alleluias.*

Bolduc describes the scene at her church one Sunday morning when her eleven-year-old son, Joel, sat between his parents on a Communion Sunday. They started taking Joel into the church worship services when he was just five. Joel suffered from a disability that sometimes created behavior issues. Sunday school was not working for him. Joel loved the services, and his spontaneity during the services took some getting used to by the other worshippers. He loved the music and would imitate the choir director, sing loudly, and end each song with an "'Amen!' . . . generally a few beats behind the rest of the congregation."[7] When they weren't singing, it was hard for Joel to sit still; he was often a distraction because they sat on the front row so that Joel would not kick the seat in front of him. "And at least once during every service [he] says in a loud voice, 'I have to go to the bathroom!'"[8]

Bolduc writes,

On the first Sunday of the month, communion is served. We pass the bread along the pews, administering it to one another, saying, "This is the body of Jesus, broken for you." Likewise, we pass the wine to one another with the words, "This is Jesus' blood, shed that you might live." My husband and I allow Joel to take a piece of bread, reciting the familiar words to which he never seems to pay attention. He chews the bread, picking at the sticky stuff left in his teeth with his fingers, but far prefers the wine, which in our church is really grape juice. Again, we recite the words to him. "Joel, this is Jesus' blood, shed for you." He slurps down the juice and sticks his tongue into the cup, determined to get every last drop.[9]

On a particular Sunday, when the pastor read the words of institution, "This is my body" and "This is my blood," and added the phrases, "broken for you" and "shed for you," Joel stood from his seat and proclaimed, "For me!" He turned around to face the people and repeated, "For me! For me!"[10] His proud mother describes the moment: "Ordinary time stopped. All that existed in that moment was the radiant look of understanding on Joel's face. Joel knew that God loved him. . . . All the accumulated Sunday hours of embarrassment, impatience, frustration, and yearning for wholeness as the world knows wholeness sloughed away as I watched the love of God glimmer like gold in the face of my son."[11]

Discussion Questions

1. How does Jesus' example aid our perspective on those with disabilities?

2. How would you preach on the issues involved?

3. What assets and strengths does your church already have that could positively impact those with disabilities? Any weaknesses to overcome?

4. What are some steps your church could take to ready for such ministries?

Recommended Reading

Bolduc, Kathleen Deyer. *Autism and Alleluias.* Valley Forge, PA: Judson Press, 2010.

_____. *His Name Is Joel: Searching for God in a Son's Disability.* Louisville, KY: Bridge Resources, 1999.

_____. *A Place Called Acceptance: Ministry with Families of Children with Disabilities.* Louisville, KY: Bridge Resources, 2001.

Webb-Mitchell, Brett. *Unexpected Guests at God's Banquet: Welcoming People with Disabilities in the Church.* New York: Crossroad Publishing, 1994.

Young, Amos. *The Bible, Disability, and the Church.* Grand Rapids: Eerdmans, 2011.

Young, Francis. *Brokenness and Blessing: Toward a Biblical Spirituality.* Grand Rapids: Baker Academics, 2007.

fourteen
WESLEYAN CONTEXTUALIZATION
PASTORAL PRACTICES IN A MULTICULTURAL WORLD

◦◦◦

Mario Zani and Carol Rotz

Should a Latino believer living in the U.S. feel a responsibility to share the good news with people from another culture, including English locals? With the Great Commission of Jesus Christ in mind, the answer is obvious. It is the responsibility of all Christian believers, whatever their culture, to share Christ with others.

We may know the right answer; we may even be able to quote Matt. 28:21-22, but few churches reflect the rich multicultural flavor of their area's demographics.[1] Part of the problem is our view of who our world includes. Our task "to make Christlike disciples in the nations" begins in our own "Jerusalem,"[2] but many of us live isolated lives within a group of people with whom we feel comfortable. We may not even know our neighbors, so how can we share the good news with them? Telling others is limited to those with whom we have relationships. Of course, relational evangelism is essential.[3] The problem is that many are ignored because they are not part of our group. Their otherness excludes them from our lives and our churches.

Jesus told the story of a good Samaritan (Luke 10:25-37) to an expert in the Law who knew the right answer (vv. 27, 28, 37), and he charged the man to "Go and do likewise" (v. 37). We know the story.

160

We admire the Samaritan and may even cringe at the likeness of the priest and Levite to our own reactions to those in need. But do we really understand the impact of the story? We live in multicultural communities.[4] We may tolerate, even celebrate culturally distinctive food, dress, music, and other outward expressions of culture. But do we build bridges of relationship between our cultural communities by sharing, listening, and learning?[5] Note that the Samaritan in Jesus' story is not the object of compassion but the example to be emulated. The beauty of an intercultural church is the new perspectives and opportunities to grow more and more like God's "kingdom . . . as it is in heaven" (Matt. 6:10).

More than a Definition

A reading of John Wesley's *Works* as well as his biography led me (Zani) many years ago to the conclusion that his theology derives from the Word of God.[6] It is *practical* in nature and essence, *present* (incarnational) in this world, *pertinent* to any context, and *productive* in positive changes internally for the church and externally to the other. All of these inform this chapter on intercultural ministry, but space does not allow an exploration of them. We will look at only one example.

In his sermon "Of the Church,"[7] Wesley reminds us that the church is not a building but a people. More than forty years of ministry in different levels of the church in many world areas compels me to humbly reflect on this fundamental reality from my own context.[8] In this sermon Wesley answers the question, what is the church? And this is where we must begin if we are to fulfill the Great Commission. Wesley affirms the biblical foundation of the article of faith embraced by the English church of his time, but he emphasizes that answering the question is more than just providing a theologically elaborate and sophisticated definition for church leadership to affirm. Ultimately we will be judged not by our definition but by our praxis.

What we biblically define as church—its essence, attitude, and behavior—should, Wesley writes, be reflected at all times. It should produce spiritual growth in the congregation, but it should also effect change in the surrounding community. This last aspect is a forgotten task. The risk always exists for the church to practice only what benefits the local congregation without much reflection on the scriptural call to truly impact its cultural context—persons and community in need of God. We cannot forget that at the birth of the church linguistic and national boundaries were exploded (Acts 2:5-6) and that the vision of the church is a countless multitude "from every nation, tribe, people and language" (Rev. 7:9).

More than Generalities

The reality comes into focus when faces are superimposed over the collective picture. One day I was visiting with one of the first members of our new Hispanic ministry.

"Pastor, I was a hypocrite during the years I attended church. I attended church during the first three years after you and your wife started the Hispanic congregation. You and your wife challenged us to be trained in our faith, but because of a lack of responsibility on my part I skipped or avoided the opportunities. You graciously allowed me to sing almost every Sunday. Pastor, I was somewhat open to 'do' Christian things, but my interest never was in deepening my knowledge of God, his Word, and his will for me and my family."

With tears in his eyes Victor kept repeating about how he did not pay attention to the things that matter the most. "I fell into sin, and I am so sorry. I know the Lord has forgiven me; I asked him for that. And now, all is different. I realize that I missed opportunities to be a faithful Christian in the past, to listen and try to understand the preaching and what was taught in Bible studies. But since receiving the Bible you sent me I have begun to seriously read, meditate, and study it. More than that, Pastor, a Bible study group has been formed. Sixteen have already accepted Christ during the last three months. We are meeting every day for prayer and Bible study. Pastor, if I had realized before . . . I was hypocrite; I've been a fool."

We prayed together and it was time for me to leave. Back in my car in the prison parking lot I put my head on the steering wheel and with tears in my eyes I prayed, "Lord, I know there's something I have to change. As a pastor, I cannot just blame people like Victor. There's something I'm not doing well as a pastor. I thoroughly prepare for each Sunday service. I strive for each lesson to be clearly presented and for the students to participate in class. But something is not right." As a church we failed this man who was in the Washington County prison awaiting trial for a serious crime.

I look at his experience as a mirror of all we do as pastors and churches. Where do we fail people like Victor—people who do not fit the culture of a local church? It is not always language or ethnicity but other factors that hinder growth. How do we make them feel not just welcome but a vital part of the body where they can grow into the persons God has created them to be?

Part of the problem is that we define Christian worship too narrowly. We do all the right things, each in their allotted time, at least in the eyes of the dominant culture. But much of what we do may seem strange to those with different backgrounds. All is familiar to us, and we assume it is the right way to do it, but people with different perceptions, priorities, and assumptions may find it strange and uncomfortable.

Let's return to Wesley's sermon. In it he explains that the church should walk in a manner worthy of our vocation. In humility, meekness, long-suffering, and love we are to build a church united in peace (Eph. 4:1-3). The implications for intercultural ministry are staggering.

More than a Building

Even when our worship services are truly intercultural it is all too easy to walk out of the church building and forget that we are still the body of Christ on earth. Our walk in the world should of course be consistent with our Christian identity, which includes our thinking, speaking, and acting. This is not a small thing. But do we remember our ultimate motivation? It is not to show the world we are good Christians! It is to show the world the love of Christ in such a way and in such a degree that our communities actually change because we are present and active in them.

We have missed the point if we remain aloof from the world outside our doors. Whether ordinary people, immigrants, marginalized or privileged, everyone is worthy to receive the message of salvation. God will ask us for each one. There are many that need to be saved, and we are responsible to share the message intentionally, diligently, and efficiently with them. This is overwhelming. How can we reach those we don't understand, don't relate to, and don't know? How can we become truly intercultural?

The beginning of an answer is obvious. We need to ask! To fulfill an intercultural class assignment to spend five hours with a person from another culture one student interacted with a person he had worked with for five years. He knew she was not a native of Idaho but knew nothing beyond that—not even her name. Their families got together for a traditional Peruvian meal, and friendships were formed. It was a beginning. He learned to celebrate another's food, music, and stories. As a church we need to be even more intentional because behaviors, traditions, and customs are only the surface aspects of culture. Like an iceberg, they represent only about 10 percent of a culture. Core values, beliefs, priorities, attitudes, assumptions, and perceptions lie beneath the surface and are much more difficult to be aware of, much less understand.[9]

We need to go beneath the surface and become fluent in others' values, beliefs, and ways of looking at life. This is especially true for those who are part of the racial, ethnic, and cultural majority. Historically the church has too often confused gospel values with those of the dominant culture, limiting or even distorting our understanding of the gospel. Other perspectives will enrich our church, for they have much to teach us and we have much to learn. And as we learn we can minister more effectively to all in our communities.

Fulfilling the Great Commission includes more than supporting a missionary program, as important as that is. It is basic to who we are as a church and includes such things as our finances, compassion, and evangelism.

A church's budget reveals its true priorities whatever its mission statement might say. We never have enough money to do all we would like, but finances should not be used as an excuse for a local church not to reach out to all in the community. The argument of limited finances has proven to be without foundation biblically and historically. If a calculator is what determines the degree of impact the church can make in its community, sooner or later that church will be diminished and wiped out from its midst.

The foundational necessity is that the church—the congregation and the pastor—should experience a constant transformation to the likeness of Christ. Reaching others for Christ, particularly those living in the diverse multicultural world our communities have become, is a matter of the stewardship of the church's resources. And the church's greatest resource is the people themselves. It is important to note that stewardship includes much more than material resources and church program participation. Some members may think that because they spend time at church they are good stewards; others, because they exercise their talents in the church may feel they have fulfilled their stewardship. Others, because they pay their offerings, tithes, and support projects with their treasures or economic resources, may feel they are good stewards. All of these are important but not the central aspects of stewardship. Every member should be prepared and mobilized to impact the community. This includes developing cultural intelligence—

being aware of our own culture and those of the people God has placed within our sphere of influence.

Community-oriented churches that reflect the sociodemographic makeup of the locality are difficult to achieve.[10] It is costly to include everyone. Both financial and human resources are stretched to accomplish the goal of inclusivity. Many middle-class churches, for example, find it difficult to create a comfortable place for others less fortunate. Compassion is not absent but often remains with an us-them mentality that cares for those in need but does not include them in the family. On a Saturday morning I (Zani) was teaching a class at the gym of a local church and I heard a little of the story of one of the ladies handing out bags of food to the needy. She had assisted the church with the distribution of food for five years. She loved doing it mostly because it was a way to help her own family, but she shared with me that she was not a Christian. I asked if anyone had told her about Christ, and her answer spoke volumes. "No," she said, "I do not think so. I do not remember."

There is no one model for ministering in a multicultural world. The essential ingredients are awareness, intentionality, and adaptability. It is a matter of the church being the church so that everyone can see, hear, and have the opportunity to accept Christ and be his faithful follower. There will not be an issue of race, creed, color, preference, or status. The message of the church will be shared with all, and all will feel welcome to join the church—as in New Testament and Wesley's times.

> O "let your light shine before men!" Show them your faith by your works. Let them see, by the whole tenor of your conversation, that your hope is all laid up above! Let all your words and actions evidence the spirit whereby you are animated! Above all things let your love abound. Let it extend to every child of man: Let it overflow to every child of God. By this let all men know whose disciples ye are, because you "love one another."[11]

Discussion Questions

1. Read Wesley's sermon, "Of the Church" <http://wesley.nnu. edu/john-wesley/the-sermons-of-john-wesley-1872-edition/>. Choose and discuss a couple of his sermon statements and compare them with the state of your church today. How do they impact a multicultural community?

2. What are three major challenges you face in making the church relevant in your community? Explain.

3. Think about some of the instances when you shared your faith with nonbelievers in your community. Describe how you approached them (steps), their response, your reactions, and how you followed up the contact you made with them.

4. Who represents "the other" for you? To which culture or subculture do you find it hardest to relate? Analyze the stereotypes of this group and the negativity of such generalizations. What stereotypes do others have of your identity group?

5. What cultures (linguistic, socioeconomic, ethnic, generational) are represented in your church? What is the dominant culture? Are other perspectives acknowledged, encouraged, celebrated? Why or why not? What would have to happen for there to be change?

6. What models of evangelism and church growth does your church employ to fulfill the Great Commission? Are you reaching all sectors of your community? Is it a matter of awareness, priorities, or something else?

Recommended Reading

Appleby, Jerry, with Glen Van Dyne. *The Church Is in a Stew: Developing Multicongregational Churches.* Kansas City: Beacon Hill Press of Kansas City, 1990.

Conde-Frazier, Elizabeth, S. Steve Kang, and Gary A. Parrett. *A Many Colored Kingdom: Multicultural Dynamics for Spiritual Formation.* Grand Rapids: Baker Academic, 2004.

Conn, Harvie M., ed. *Planting and Growing Urban Churches: From Dream to Reality.* Grand Rapids: Baker Book House, 1997.

Kruschwitz, Robert B. *Immigration: Christian Reflection.* Waco, TX: Baylor University, 2008.

Livermore, David A. *Cultural Intelligence: Improving Your CQ to Engage Our Multicultural World.* Grand Rapids: Baker Academic, 2009.

Milne, Bruce. *Dynamic Diversity: Bridging Class, Age, Race, and Gender in the Church.* Downers Grove, IL: InterVarsity Press, 2007.

Phillips, Oliver R., ed. *E Pluribus Unum: Challenges and Opportunities in Multicultural Ministry.* Kansas City: Beacon Hill Press of Kansas City, 2007.

Rankin, Jerry. *Empowering Kingdom Growth to the Ends of the Earth: Churches Fulfilling the Great Commission.* Nashville: Broadman and Holman, 2006.

Zani, Mario J. "Ministering in the Latino Community." Online: <http://www.culturalexpressionsmag.net/articles/ministering-in-the-latino-community>.

fifteen

CASE STUDY
WESLEYAN PRACTICAL THEOLOGY AT WORK IN THE CITY

~~◦

Jon Middendorf

Oklahoma City is one of the five largest cities in the world—though by "largest" I mean area, not population. "Oklahoma City covers 622 square miles—more than Houston, Atlanta, or even New York City."[1] Our city sprawls in every direction, and the land grab continues as we speak. There's room to move and breathe, no question. But at the same time, the expanse raises social and societal questions, and churches like ours (Oklahoma City First) must have the sensitivity, the imagination, and the courage to at least address if not answer these questions. As Wesleyans, we already have the theological resources to order the steps of mission and ministry.

As you might expect, dreamers, the developers, and the planners push city lines farther and farther from the city's center. Forecasters predict where the city and the growth will occur; those with the deeper pockets, or access to them, pounce. Neighborhood developers, home builders, businesses, and churches compete for this newly minted prime real estate. But there are implications. I'm not suggesting that it is inherently immoral or unethical to move to the new part of town. Churches moving away from urban challenges, and into what can be described as rural/suburban settings, do alter the trajectories of both the old neighborhood and the migrating congregation itself.

Several years ago at OKC First, a group of elected and appointed leaders studied the possibility of a move to the northern, growing edge of the city. The reasons for a move seemed compelling: the church was landlocked; the congregation was (is) moving to the northern part of town; our current neighborhood was (is) deteriorating. After weeks of study and many conversations with city planners and managers, the decision was made to stay at 4400 NW Expressway—the current location of OKC First.

The reasons to stay were even more compelling: with a traffic volume of one hundred thousand cars passing daily, businesses were still attracted to the area bringing jobs and dollars, but the neighborhood around us was (is) deteriorating. At the end of the conversation, OKC First recognized the need to stay and change in order to nurture and serve both the deteriorating bedroom community *and* the still-thriving business community.

As we continued to study our city and neighborhood, we grew increasingly aware of the importance of the automobile. In such a large city with such a poor system of mass transit, cars are essential lifelines. We found this axiom to be too true—those living anywhere near the poverty line would quickly plummet beneath it if/when something goes wrong with their cars. While a myriad of issues and problems surrounds our community, this issue is one of the most significant, and the one I'll use to discuss the Wesleyan ways in which we, as a congregation, have moved against this societal sin.

I use the term "sin" intentionally. While the Western church, following Western culture, has long been fixated on the self, Wesley's understanding of sin reached far beyond the individual believer. While not disregarding the reality of individual sinfulness, Wesley appreciated that sin also functioned at relational, societal, and even ecological levels. Sin and its pervasive effects were painfully evident to Wesley as he worked tirelessly to feed the hungry or nurture the sick and dying.

At the same time, Wesley preached a doctrine of grace, which, like sin, operated on multiple levels. A discussion of grace, like sin, cannot be confined in its scope to the interior life of the individual believer. The doctrine of prevenient grace suggests that we are made in the image of God; as individuals, each of us bears the image of God— an image marred, confused, or covered up by sin. But grace continues to pursue and romance us, and when allowed to do so this same grace can restore and renew the image of God and return us to full "humanness." But again, this conversation is not meant to be confined to the plight of the individual believer.

The church, the body of Christ, the congregation of believing individuals, itself stands in need of this sanctifying grace. Having been formed to image Christ to the world, it yet suffers the debilitating effects of sin; at the same time we can know the power and promise of liberating grace. Take one more step back, allow for a larger picture to emerge and consider this: all of creation is created with a familial resemblance to Christ, the Firstborn. Creation itself can be marred, confused, or buried by sin. But sanctifying grace can operate here, too, at a societal level. Grace exposes the sins that would bring chaos and captivity and makes available the resources for help, healing, and liberation, in order that society can be renewed and God's likeness restored.

So, to recap: words like "sin," "grace," "salvation," "sanctification," and "revival" all functioned on multiple dimensions for Wesley; they will for us as well, if we are to undertake mission and ministry as Wesleyan congregations. Recognizing that these words function on individual and corporate levels simultaneously, we understand that the work done to recover God's likeness in a neighborhood at the same time brings health benefits to the body of Christ and to the individuals that make up that local body of believers. We know that we must be more than recipients of this grace; we must respond to it and cooperate with it. In so doing the reign of God (one of Wesley's favorite phrases) is furthered and continued in and through us.

As I mentioned earlier, cars are lifelines for a number of the residents of Oklahoma City. Many of those in the apartment complexes near the church have neither a car nor access to a car. In a city so spread out, this limits one's ability to find or keep a job. Without reliable transportation, life spirals out of control pretty quickly. Ironically, many struggle to find transportation to the agencies designed to provide help for folks in these exact situations!

We've noticed too that there are no grocery stores within walking distance of the church, especially when weather is an issue (as is often true where "the wind comes sweeping down the plain"). Multiply the degree of difficulty by adding a child or two or three to tow on the two-mile walk to the grocery store that's on the other side of the very busy expressway I mentioned before. (Just to make things a bit more difficult, there aren't sidewalks or bike paths that might make the trip a bit faster or safer.)

Without access to a real grocery store, our neighbors stuck in this vicious cycle shop at the closest convenience store, one that doesn't carry fruit, vegetables, or fresh meat of any kind. Even a person proactive enough to secure unemployment aid or other assistance, but without a car, might force that person to shop for groceries where there aren't any healthy choices. As you might expect, there is a physical price to be paid when nutritional needs go unmet. All of that, combined with a substandard mass leaves the alert and caring observer to conclude that the system is not only broken but tilted—tilted toward the financially comfortable, toward those with money to buy, operate, and maintain a car. But the above system does not take into account all of the working-class poor in our section of Oklahoma City.

Our response to this issue has taken a variety of forms. We have begun serving a meal on a weekly basis at two area apartment complexes considered at-risk. Every Sunday afternoon, a team of ten to twelve people serves dinner to anyone who'll walk up and take a plate. Each week we're able to connect, face-to-face, with two hundred families who are in various places of need and opportunity. As our team members become aware of needs and the plight of our new friends, we move to respond. Sometimes that response takes the form of simple car maintenance or more extensive repair work. Sometimes that work is done by those in our church with some level of automotive expertise. But sometimes a car can't be repaired, and the only answer is a different car altogether.

Recently a young woman named Stephanie, divorced and with a small child, found herself in harm's way. She was a licensed teacher, experienced and skilled, but new to the area. She finally found a teaching job, but when her car failed her, she found herself at the nearest bus stop (her daughter in tow), to board the 5 a.m. for the two-hour ride to the school, in order to be at work on time. This was not a workable, long-term solution for Stephanie, the school, or her daughter. She was just one medical bill, one pink slip away from desperation.

We announced this need to our congregation, and soon a dependable used car was gifted to the church. We made this car available to Stephanie, who is now thriving in her job. Stephanie and her daughter are faithful members of our faith community now, growing with us toward God's wholeness, health, and liberty.

These works of mercy are essential—not just for those on the receiving end but also for those who are ministering in the name of Christ and OKC First. Not coincidentally, those involved in the processes of provision and mentoring are themselves being shaped and restored. Again, recognize and appreciate that grace operates on a number of levels simultaneously. But this is a justice issue as well. As we are ministering to the "wounded," we are also taking aim at the system that wounds. We Wesleyans understand both sin and grace to be at work in this arena as well.

We have met (and will continue to meet) with those elected and appointed officials in places of supervision and leadership in our community. We are learning the systems involved where decisions are made about sidewalks, bike trails, bus stops, and bus routes. The halls of power are largely unfamiliar to us in the church (we've left that work to others in the "real world"). But we now recognize that we are called to these places as well, if in fact we have the confidence and the characteristically Wesleyan optimism that God by his grace can make a difference, even in the realm of planning and public policy.

We are working and networking with various voices in our neighborhood in the hopes of gathering a critical mass that can speak with one voice to the powers in Oklahoma City. Our neighborhood is decidedly "unpracticed" where this kind of thinking is concerned. Survival demands too much energy! Consequently, the people of our neighborhood lack the will or the imagination to make their voices heard. The city's culture will continue to leave them out of the process unless something is done, until the processes are brought to light and changed. We're helping build a neighborhood coalition that will know the system well enough to speak into it, with a decidedly Christian tone, with a decidedly Christian outcome and vision in mind. But our efforts have included pain!

This language makes some people nervous. For some reason, returning to our theological roots has resulted in many being offended . . . politically. With the fairly recent onset of the twenty-four-hour cable news networks, the professional-political-entertainment industry has enormously impacted the people in our congregations and the beliefs and convictions our people bring with them into the sanctuary.

During the 2008 presidential campaign, each candidate's political career was placed under the microscope. Soon enough it came to light that one had been involved in a community-organizing initiative whose agenda was described as partisan, divisive, and politically minded. This was used to demonize not just the candidate in question but also the words, strategies, and ideas involved in the concept of community organizing.

At the same time that war was being fought in the headlines and on the news networks, we were trying to organize our community for the continuing reign of God in our part of Oklahoma City. We tried to partner with other faith communities who shared a similar, hopeful, healthy vision for northwest Oklahoma City. But we soon found ourselves locked in a battle we hadn't foreseen or intended. We watched as the political realm reached deeply into the work and agenda of the local church, co-opting the meaning of long-respected and meaningful words and phrases like "social justice" and "social holiness." Fearing that our efforts would be misinterpreted and ultimately fruitless, we separated ourselves from any organization believed to have its own political agenda; we regrouped in hopes of accomplishing social and societal change explicitly in the name of Christ.

But we have not shied away from cooperation or collaboration. In fact, I continue to believe that we Wesleyans are hardwired for collaborative efforts. John Wesley, especially toward the end of his ministry, quite actively championed changes to public policy that would result in a healthier, more sustainable, more redemptive society. If a partnership could further or promote his ministries or his ideas without compromising Wesley's integrity or purposes, all the better!

Your local church might seem isolated and weak when you start considering the vast changes that can be made, that cry to be made in your neighborhood. That's exactly how we felt. But we have been surprised and encouraged to find many other ministries and agencies eager to partner with us in the renovation of our neighborhoods. More than once, as we have added partners to our list, we've voiced our belief that prevenient grace has been at work, behind the scenes, moving and realigning for the sake of our corner of God's creation and the glory of God.

We now find ourselves in partnership with other Christian ministries (TASK–gang prevention ministries), other community-based organizations (Community Literacy Centers) and national organizations with local interests (Big Brothers/Big Sisters). We are responding to and cooperating with God's prevenient grace; God is giving us both the vision and the connections to spread and further the kingdom.

And at the same time, we—as a church and as the individual believers in this church—are being renewed and restored. We have learned so much—most of it good! It is my best hope and prayer that our experiences and lessons might help you to be the embodiment of God's liberating grace in your neighborhood.

Discussion Questions

1. Why do churches move away from deteriorating neighborhoods?

2. Why is the discussion of sin, salvation, and sanctification so often confined to the individual believer?

3. Can you see the sins or the effect of sins at work in the neighborhood around your church? If so, how would you describe those sins?

4. What is the difference between works of mercy and acts of justice?

5. How can a church responsibly, and yet effectively, perform works of mercy and works of justice?

Recommended Reading

Berkhof, Hendrikus. *Christ and the Powers.* Waterloo, ON: Herald Press, 1977.

Collins, Kenneth. *The Theology of John Wesley: Holy Love and the Shape of Grace.* Nashville: Abingdon, 2007.

Maddox, Randy. *Responsible Grace: John Wesley's Practical Theology.* Nashville: Abingdon Press, 1994.

Wink, Walter. *Engaging the Powers: Discernment and Resistance in a World of Domination.* Minneapolis: Fortress Press, 1992.

_____. *Naming the Powers: The Language of Power in the New Testament.* Minneapolis: Fortress Press, 1984.

_____. *The Powers that Be: A Theology for a New Millennium.* New York: Three Rivers Press, 1999.

_____. *Unmasking the Powers,* Vol. 2. Minneapolis: Augsburg Fortress Publishers, 1986.

NOTES

Chapter 1

1. Randy Maddox, *Responsible Grace: John Wesley's Practical Theology* (Nashville: Abingdon Press, 1994).

2. Samual J. Rogal, "'The Elder unto the Well-beloved': The Letters of John Wesley," in *Journal of Religious Studies* 7 (Fall 1979): 74.

3. For only one example among numerous others, see John Wesley, Letter to Ann Bolton (7 April 1768), in *The Letters of John Wesley,* ed. John Telford (London: Epworth Press, 1931), 5:86, hereafter cited as *Letters* (Telford).

4. Baker remarks, "Undoubtedly [the continual increase] was in part because a larger proportion of his later letters were preserved by eager devotees, and because improved postal services had led to a general increase in letter-writing. The major factor governing this great increase during his later years, however, was surely the demands made upon Wesley's pastoral concern by a rapidly growing Methodist community, combined with his amazing vigour" (Frank Baker, ed., introduction to *Letters I: 1721-1739,* vol. 25, *The Bicentennial Edition to the Works of John Wesley* [Nashville: Abingdon, 1984—], 29, hereafter cited as *Bicentennial Works*).

5. Ibid., 30.

6. Letter to Miss Clarkson (5 April 1781), in *Letters* (Telford), 7:56.

7. The following pages represent my survey of the approximately 850 letters to women and a smaller sampling of letters to men, found in Telford's "Standard Edition" of Wesley's *Letters* (Telford's total is 2,670).

8. Rogal remarks, "Essentially, Wesley could control his male preachers, stewards, and trustees; if they failed to obey his wishes or to conduct themselves according to his strict standards, he simply moved them out of his way. However, in regard to women, he found certain situations far more difficult to settle; he found himself not always able to act as organizational administrator or spiritual leader" ("The Elder," 79).

9. See W. F. Lofthouse, "John Wesley's Letters to His Brother," *London Quarterly and Holborn Review* 185 (April 1960): 133-29.

10. Paul Chilcote examines the characterization of Wesley put forth in the personal reflections of one of these women, Hester Ann Rogers. Chilcote presents Rogers' Wesley as a deeply compassionate, intensely tender, relationally focused personality. See Paul W. Chilcote, "John Wesley as revealed by the Journal of Hester Ann Rogers, July 1775—October 1784," in *Methodist History* 20

(1982): 111-23. I would suggest that while he does present himself similarly in the majority of his letters to women, the intensity of Wesley's "focus" (i.e., "gaze") could elicit a much more negative interpretation of aspects of his personality.

11. E.g., Hannah Ball, Ann Bolton, Mary (Bosanquet) Fletcher, Sarah Crosby, Lady Maxwell, Emma Moon.

12. Rogal, "The Elder," 75.

13. John Wesley, *The Works of John Wesley*, ed. Thomas Jackson (1872; repr., Kansas City: Beacon Hill Press of Kansas City, 1986), 10:480, hereafter cited as *Works* (Jackson).

14. See Richard Heitzenrater, *Wesley and the People Called Methodists* (Nashville: Abingdon Press, 1995), 182-98.

15. Thomas Langford, "John Wesley and Theological Method," in *Rethinking Wesley's Theology for Contemporary Methodism*, ed. Randy Maddox (Nashville: Abingdon Press, 1998), 47.

16. Randy Maddox, "John Wesley: Practical Theologian?" in *Wesleyan Theological Journal* 23 (1988): 122-47.

17. Ibid., 134.

18. Franz Hildebrandt, *Christianity According to the Wesleys* (Grand Rapids: Baker Books, 1996), 31. Originally published by Epworth Press, London, 1956.

19. Langford, "John Wesley and Theological Method," 35.

20. Ibid., 125.

21. Ibid.

22. Ibid., 47.

23. Ibid., 37.

24. Mark A. Maddix, *Reflecting John Wesley's Theology and Educational Perspective: Comparing Nazarene Pastors, Christian Educators, and Professors of Christian Education* (Ph.D. diss., Spring Arbor: UMI), 220.

25. Ibid.

26. Ibid., 225.

Chapter 2

1. William J. Abraham, "Wesley as Preacher," in *The Cambridge Companion to John Wesley*, eds. Randy L. Maddox and Jason E. Vickers (New York: Cambridge University Press, 2010), 98. For an incisive discussion of Wesley's preaching ministry within the broader context of his magisterial study of the history of Christian preaching, see Hughes Oliphant Old, "John Wesley," in *The Reading and Preaching of the Scriptures in the Worship of the Christian Church*, vol. 5, *Moderatism, Pietism, and Awakening* (Grand Rapids: Eerdmans, 2004), 110-35.

2. John Wesley, preface to *Sermons on Several Occasions*, vol. 1 (1746), para. 5, in *Bicentennial Works*, 1:104-5.

3. Randy L. Maddox, "The Rule of Christian Faith, Practice, and Hope: John Wesley on the Bible," published in *Methodist Review: A Journal of Wesleyan and Methodist Studies* 3 (2011): 1-35. ISSN: 1946-5254 (online) <www.methodist review.org>.

4. Maddox, "John Wesley on the Bible," 1. See also Thomas C. Oden, *John Wesley's Scriptural Christianity: A Plain Exposition of His Teaching on Christian Doctrine* (Grand Rapids: Zondervan, 1994), 59: "'Every good textuary is a good divine,' and 'none can be a good Divine who is not a good textuary.'"

5. Richard P. Heitzenrater, "John Wesley's Principles and Practice of Preaching," in *Methodist History* 37, no. 2 (January 1999), 103. Heitzenrater goes on to report Wesley's later scolding of the Methodist preachers who took his earlier comment on "the one book" to its literal conclusion by apparently refusing to read anything other than the Bible. Accusing such preachers of laziness, Wesley advocates constant reading as the antidote to ignorance in the pulpit: "Read the most useful books, and that regularly and constantly . . . *at least five hours* [italics mine] in twenty-four."

6. Maddox, "John Wesley on the Bible," 16.

7. Robin Scroggs, "John Wesley as Biblical Scholar," in *Journal of Bible and Religion* 28, no. 4, 415-22.

8. See Anna Carter Florence, "Put Away Your Sword!" in *What's the Matter with Preaching Today?* Mike Graves, ed. (Louisville, KY: Westminster John Knox Press, 2004), 93-108.

9. See Old, "John Wesley," 114: "Wesley used a certain number of sermons over and over again. He carefully wrote them out early in his ministry and adapted them to particular situations as occasion demanded. As time went along these 'standard sermons' were published with the intention that they would define the teaching of the Methodist movement."

10. Florence, "Put Away Your Sword!" 98-99.

11. Eugene H. Peterson, *Eat This Book: A Conversation in the Art of Spiritual Reading* (Grand Rapids: Eerdmans, 2006), 57.

12. Richard P. Heitzenrater, *Mirror and Memory: Reflections on Early Methodism* (Nashville: Abingdon Press, 1989), 163. See also Old, "John Wesley," 111.

13. Heitzenrater, "Principles and Practice of Preaching," 93-94. Heitzenrater goes on to note that Whitefield certainly recognized the disparity between the longer term results of his ministry and that of Wesley, quoting Whitefield: "My brother Wesley acted wisely. The souls that were awakened under his ministry he joined in class, and thus preserved the fruit of his labour. This I neglected and my people are a rope of sand." Heitzenrater also reports that in 1770, Wesley commented to much the same effect in the "Large" *Minutes* (*Minutes of the Methodist Conferences* [London: John Mason, 1862], 1:470): "It is far easier to preach a good sermon than to instruct the ignorant in the principles of religion."

14. Quoted in W. L. Doughty, *John Wesley: Preacher* (London: Epworth, 1955), 194.

15. See Wesley, "Letter on Preaching Christ" (20 December 1751), in *Works* (Jackson), 11:486-92. See also the comment on this correspondence and its underlying issue for the developing Methodist societies in Heitzenrater, *Wesley and the People Called Methodists*, 185.

16. Mildred B. Wynkoop, "A Wesleyan View on Preaching Holiness," *Wesleyan Theological Journal* 4, no. 1 (Spring 1969), 18.

17. Daniel L. Burnett, *In the Shadow of Aldersgate: An Introduction to the Heritage and Faith of the Wesleyan Tradition* (Eugene, OR: Cascade Books, 2006), 113.

18. Thomas G. Long, *Preaching from Memory to Hope* (Louisville, KY: Westminster John Knox Press, 2009), 91-92.

19. Old, "John Wesley," 128.

Chapter 3

1. The author is thinking of several occasions over the past twenty-five years where sacraments have been occasioned as "big moments" in the life of the church. On one such occasion a noted preacher and teacher of the Wesleyan tradition preached his sermon and then sat down. After a few minutes he called upon the congregation to come to the Lord's Table to eat and drink as they wanted. There was no invitation given; no words of institution; no words of consecration; no calling to mind of the suffering, death, and resurrection of Jesus Christ. It was literally a meal with no purpose.

2. Wesley, "The Means of Grace," in *Bicentennial Works*, 1:381.

3. Wesley, "A Treatise on Baptism," in *Works* (Jackson), 10:188.

4. Laurence Hull Stookey, "Methodism and the Sacraments," in *T&T Clark Companion to Methodism*, ed. Charles Yrigoyen Jr. (New York: T&T Clark International, 2010), 259.

5. Ibid.

6. Geoffrey Wainwright, "The Sacraments," in *The Oxford Handbook of Methodist Studies*, eds. William J. Abraham and James E. Kirby (New York: Oxford University Press, 2009), 345.

7. Ibid.

8. William H. Willimon, "Acts," in *Interpretation: A Bible Commentary for Teaching and Preaching* (Atlanta: John Knox Press, 1988), 37.

9. Ibid., 38.

10. Rob L. Staples, *Outward Sign and Inward Grace: The Place of Sacraments in Wesleyan Spirituality* (Kansas City: Beacon Hill Press of Kansas City, 1992), 122.

11. Wesley, "Treatise on Baptism," in *Works* (Jackson), 10:190.

12. Ibid., 194.

13. Ibid., 195.

14. Ibid., 196.

15. Ibid.

16. Ibid.

17. Staples, *Outward Sign and Inward Grace*, 202.

18. Wainwright, "The Sacraments," 350.

19. Wesley, journal entry (28 June 1740), in *Bicentennial Works*, 19:159.

20. Ibid.

21. Stookey, "Methodism and the Sacraments," 266.

22. Ibid.

23. Ibid., 263.

24. These are the words of invitation traditionally used by churches in the Wesleyan Methodist tradition.

Chapter 4

1. Johann Arndt, *True Christianity*, trans. Peter Erb (New York: Paulist, 1979), 21.

2. M. Robert Mulholland Jr., *Invitation to a Journey: A Road Map for Spiritual Formation* (Downers Grove, IL: InterVarsity, 1993), 15.

3. Wesley, "A Word to a Methodist," para. 3, in *Bicentennial Works*, 9:244; "Reasons Against a Separation from the Church of England," para. III.2, in *Bicentennial Works*, 9:339; and Sermon 84, "The Important Question," para. III.1, in *Bicentennial Works*, 3:189.

4. Maddox, *Responsible Grace*, 205.

5. Thomas C. Oden, *Pastoral Theology: Essentials of Ministry* (New York: HarperCollins, 1983), 88.

6. Ibid., 89.

7. Ibid.

8. Ibid., 90.

9. Maddox, *Responsible Grace*, 209.

10. Ibid.

11. John Calvin, *Institutes of the Christian Religion*, ed. J. T. McNeill. 2 vols. (1559 edition), para. 4.3.

12. Oden speaks more deeply on preaching and its impact on changed behavior in *Pastoral Theology*. Refer to chap. 9. Wesley's major studies on the practice of preaching are in Doughty, *John Wesley: Preacher*; and Albert C. Outler, ed., *Sermons*, vols. 1-4, *Bicentennial Works*.

13. Maddox, *Responsible Grace*, 208.

14. Robert E. Webber, *Ancient-Future Time: Forming Spirituality Through the Christian Year* (Grand Rapids: Baker Books, 2004), 31. Webber has written

the *Ancient-Future* series and provides a wonderfully articulate introduction and structure to forming spirituality through the Christian year. Titles include *Ancient-Future Faith; Ancient-Future Evangelism; Ancient-Future Time.*

15. Maddox, *Responsible Grace*, 207.

16. Ibid., 210.

17. Ibid.

18. Luke 4:18-19.

19. Mulholland, *Invitation to a Journey*, 158.

Chapter 5

1. John Telford, *The Life of John Wesley*, Chapter 10. (Retrieved October 10, 2011, at <http://wesley.nnu.edu/?id=92, 12>.)

2. John H. Westerhoff III, *Living the Faith Community* (Minneapolis: Winston Press, 1985), 27.

3. William Willimon, *Pastor, the Theology and Practice of Ordained Ministry* (Nashville: Abingdon Press, 2002), 315.

Chapter 6

1. Mildred Bangs Wynkoop, *A Theology of Love* (Kansas City: Beacon Hill Press of Kansas City, 1972), 56.

2. Ibid.

3. Ibid., 61.

4. Ibid., 54.

5. Ibid.

6. Ibid., 166.

7. Ibid.

8. Ibid., 169.

9. Carl Rogers, *Client-Centered Therapy: Its Current Practice, Implications, and Theory* (London: Constable Publishers, 2003).

10. Gerald Corey, *Theory and Practice of Counseling and Psychotherapy* (Pacific Grove, CA: Brooks/Cole Publishing, 1991), 215.

11. Wynkoop, *Theology of Love*, 81.

12. Ibid., 82.

13. Wesley, "Predestination Calmly Considered," in *Works* (Jackson), 10:223.

14. Wesley, Letter to Mrs. Bennis (16 June 1772), in *Letters* (Telford), 5:322.

15. Wynkoop, *Theology of Love*, 202.

16. Ibid., 87.

17. Ibid., 141.

18. Ibid., 142.

Chapter 7

1. Known as John Wesley's Rule.

2. Manfred Marquardt, *John Wesley's Social Ethics, Praxis and Principles* (Nashville: Abingdon Press, 1992), 103.

3. Diane Leclerc, *Discovering Christian Holiness: The Heart of Wesleyan-Holiness Theology* (Kansas City: Beacon Hill Press of Kansas City, 2010), 275.

4. Department of Preventive Medicine at the University of Kansas, School of Medicine (accessed September 30, 2011).

5. Maddox, *Responsible Grace*, 68.

6. Duke Divinity School, *The Clergy Health Initiative* <http://divinity.duke.edu/initiatives-centers/clergy-health-initiative> (accessed September 23, 2011).

7. Chinese proverb, origin unknown.

8. Ronald Koteskey <www.missionarycare.com>, 2011.

9. Wesley, "Heaviness through Manifold Temptation," in *Works* (Jackson), 6:95.

10. Duke Divinity School, *The Clergy Health Initiative* <http://divinity.duke.edu/initiatives-centers/clergy-health-initiative> (accessed September 23, 2011).

11. Ibid.

12. Wesley, "Thoughts on Nervous Disorders," in *Works* (Jackson), 11:520.

13. Roy Oswald, *Clergy Self-Care: Finding a Balance for Effective Ministry* (Herndon, VA: Alban Press, 1991), Introduction.

14. As told to Dr. Jeffrey Zeig, founder of the Milton H. Erickson Foundation.

15. The Fuller Institute of Church Growth Survey of Pastors.

16. T. Rath and D. Clifton, *How Full Is Your Bucket?* (New York: Gallup Press, 2005), 15.

17. Henri Nouwen, *Reaching Out: The Three Movements of Spiritual Life* (New York: Doubleday, 1975).

18. Gary Chapman, *The Five Languages of Love* (Chicago: Northfield Publishing, 1995).

19. The Search Institute, Minneapolis.

20. Gerard Egan, *The Skilled Helper*, 9th ed. (Belmont, CA: Brooks/Cole, 2007), 134.

Chapter 8

1. Robert Greenleaf is founder and inspiration for the Greenleaf Center. His essays on servant leadership provide an excellent description of this "servant first" approach to leadership. See Robert Greenleaf, *Servant Leadership: A Journey into the Nature of Legitimate Power and Greatness*, 3rd ed. (Mahwah, NJ: Paulist Press, 2002).

2. Kent M. Keith, *The Case for Servant Leadership* (Westfield, IN: Greenleaf Center for Servant Leadership, 2008), 11.

3. For a careful discussion of this theological reality see N. T. Wright, *Surprised by Hope: Rethinking Heaven, the Resurrection, and the Mission of the Church* (San Francisco: Harper Collins, 2008).

Chapter 9

1. For a critique of the dangers of visionary dreaming, see Dietrich Bonhoeffer, *Life Together,* trans. John W. Doberstein (San Francisco: Harper and Row, 1954), 26-31.

2. The word "pastoral" is used here not in the sense of what a pastor does, but in the sense of the care and spiritual direction of the congregation resulting from the efforts of *both* clergy and lay members of the church.

3. For a brief discussion of the term, see James E. Means, "The Purpose of Management," in *Leadership Handbook of Management and Administration,* ed. James D. Berkley (Grand Rapids: Baker Books, 2007), 352-53.

4. Robert D. Dale, "Managing Christian Institutions," in *Church Administration Handbook* (Nashville: Broadman Press, 1985), 11-12.

5. Leonard Sweet, *AquaChurch: Essential Leadership Arts for Piloting Your Church in Today's Fluid Culture* (Loveland, CO: Group Publishing, 1999), 8.

6. Albert C. Outler, "The Wesleyan Quadrilateral—in John Wesley," in *Wesleyan Theological Journal* 20:1 (1985), 7.

7. A cursory glance at the minutes of conferences meeting in the years following evidence the fact that such regulation remained a priority.

8. James D. Anderson and Ezra Earl Jones, *The Management of Ministry: Building Leadership in a Changing World* (New York: Harper and Row, 1978), 114.

9. In his sermon "The Means of Grace," John Wesley explains, "By 'means of grace' I understand outward signs, words, or actions ordained of God, and appointed for this end—to be the *ordinary* channels whereby he might convey to men preventing, justifying, or sanctifying grace. I use this expression, 'means of grace,' because I know none better, and because it . . . teaches us that a sacrament is 'an outward sign of inward *grace,* and a *means* whereby we receive the same'" (*Bicentennial Works,* 1:381).

10. The term—though not this specific application—is borrowed from Dale, "Managing Christian Institutions," 12.

11. Alvin Lindgren and Norman Shawchuck, *Management for Your Church,* cited by Henry Klopp in *The Ministry Playbook: Strategic Planning for Effective Churches* (Grand Rapids: Baker, 2002), 18.

12. Carolyn J. Cordery, "Hallowed Treasures: Sacred, Secular and the Wesleyan Methodists in New Zealand 1819-1840," Paper no. 39, *Working Paper*

Series <http://papers.ssrn.com/sol3/papers.cfm?abstract_id=1150427> (accessed October 3, 2011), 7-9.

13. "Christian tradition" refers to the historic and time-honored beliefs and practices of the Christian church.

14. John Wesley, "Preface," *Hymns and Sacred Poems* (London: printed by William Strahan, 1739), para. 5, viii.

15. Bradley W. Bateman, "The Social Gospel and the Progressive Era," *Divining America: Religion in American History* <http://nationalhumanitiescenter .org/tserve/twenty/tkeyinfo/socgospel.htm> (accessed October 5, 2011).

16. Wesley, *Hymns and Sacred Poems* (1739), para. 3, v-vi.

17. Ibid., v-viii.

18. In his sermon, "The Use of Money," Wesley reminded his audience, "When the Possessor of heaven and earth brought you into being, and placed you in this world, he placed you here, not as a proprietor, but a steward: As such he entrusted you, for a season, with goods of various kinds; but the sole property of these still rests in him, nor can ever be alienated from him" (*Bicentennial Works,* 2:277).

19. Ibid., 2:273-79.

20. See John Wesley's response to the Lord Bishop of London (June 11, 1747), in *Works* (Jackson), 8:489.

21. One of the early Rules of the Society was that "the members thereof should constantly attend the church and sacrament." See John Wesley's letter, "To the Printer of the Dublin Chronicle" (June 2, 1789), in *Works* (Jackson), 13:269.

22. In the history of Methodism in Great Britain, Wesley's administration of his societies resulted in a strength and perpetuation that never took hold among the Calvinistic Methodist societies that lacked the attention to connection despite their common theological ground.

23. Examples of the interrelationship of these three facets of the Wesleyan paradigm abound. In the Model Deed of 1763, Wesley directly connected the use of Methodist preaching houses to a commitment to continued faithfulness to the essentials of Methodist doctrine. This action has continued to influence Wesleyan approaches to church administration into the twenty-first century. See Thomas C. Oden, "The Trust Clause Governing Use of Property in the United Methodist Church: Faithfulness to the Connection According to Established Doctrinal Standards" <http://ucmpage.org/articles/oden-property.pdf> (accessed October 5, 2011). Another example is the attention the conferences gave to caring for "worn-out preachers" and to the widows and children of deceased preachers. Provision was also made to garner support for the Kingswood School, an educational enterprise of the early Methodists. See John Wesley, "Minutes of Several Conversations," in *Works* (Jackson), 8:333-34.

Chapter 10

1. Dallas Willard, *Renovation of the Heart: Putting On the Character of Christ* (Colorado Springs, CO: NavPress, 2002), 233.

2. Lecture, fall 2005, Tennessee District ordination course "Becoming Holy People."

3. John Wesley, preface to *Sermons on Several Occasions* (1771), para. 5 <http://www.swartzentrover.com/cotor/E-Books/holiness/Wesley/Sermons /JWSindex.htm>.

4. Quoted in Wes Tracy, et al., *Reflecting God* (Kansas City: Beacon Hill Press of Kansas City, 2000).

5. See Albert L. Winseman, "The 'Bottom Line' on Congregational Engagement" (October 8, 2002) <www.gallup.com>.

6. See Congregational Engagement Index Survey in "Congregational Engagement Ascends" (February 15, 2005) <www.gallup.com>.

7. Lecture, Fall 2005, Tennessee District ordination course, "Becoming Holy People."

8. A private conversation with Millard Reed.

9. I would like to pay tribute to the friend and mentor who has *most* influenced my thinking and practice as a pastor. My senior pastor, Rev. Howard L. Plummer, has modeled the way for me these last ten years. He works very hard to maintain a biblical theology that informs everything we do at Hermitage Church of the Nazarene. His preaching shapes us. He is thoroughly Wesleyan, having also been trained by great Wesley scholars such as Mildred Bangs Wynkoop, William Greathouse, H. Ray Dunning, and Millard Reed. We begin every New Year with a Wesleyan Covenant Service! He leads our pastoral staff team to work very thoughtfully and synergistically. It is a pleasure and a privilege to serve with him in such a healthy local church.

Chapter 11

1. Heitzenrater, *Wesley and the People Called Methodists*, 97.

2. Ibid., 99.

3. Ibid., 105.

4. John Wesley, "On Working Out Our Own Salvation," in *John Wesley's Sermons: An Anthology*, eds. Albert C. Outler and Richard P. Heitzenrater (Nashville: Abingdon Press, 1987), 490.

5. John Wesley, "On Visiting the Sick," Sermon 98. Available at the Wesley Center Online <http://wesley.nnu.edu/john-wesley/the-sermons-of-john-wesley -1872-edition/sermon-98-on-visiting-the-sick/> (accessed October 3, 2011).

6. Ibid.

7. Ibid.

8. Wesley, "Upon Our Lord's Sermon on the Mount, VIII," in *Works* (Jackson), 5:376-77.

Chapter 12

1. Robert Fulghum, *It Was on Fire When I Lay Down on It* (New York: Ivy Books, 1991), 191-92.

2. Wesley, "On Working Out Our Own Salvation," in *Works* (Jackson), 6:509.

3. Rob Bell, *Velvet Elvis: Re-Painting the Christian Faith* (Grand Rapids: Zondervan, 2006), 87-88.

4. Randy L. Maddox, "John Wesley and Eastern Orthodoxy: Influences, Convergences, and Differences," in *Asbury Theological Journal*, 45.2 (1990): 29-53.

5. Leonard Sweet, *A Cup of Coffee at the Soul Café* (Nashville: Broadman, 1998), 59.

6. Ibid., 64.

7. Ibid., 65.

8. Ibid., 69-70.

9. Brian D. McLaren, *More Ready than You Realize: Evangelism as a Dance in the Postmodern Matrix* (Grand Rapids: Zondervan, 2002), 15-16.

Chapter 13

1. Jennie Weiss Block, *Copious Hosting: A Theology of Access for People with Disabilities* (New York: Continuum, 2002), 32.

2. Thomas Reynolds, *Vulnerable Communion: A Theology of Disability and Hospitality* (Grand Rapids: Brazos Press, 2008), 256.

3. Ibid.

4. Jim Pierson, *Special Needs, Special Ministry for Children's Ministry* (Loveland, CO: Group Publishing, 2004), 10.

5. Nancy L. Eiesland, *The Disabled God: Toward a Liberatory Theology of Disability* (Nashville: Abingdon Press, 1994), 13.

6. Diane Leclerc, "Holiness and Power: Toward a Wesleyan Theology of Dis-ability" (The 2008 WTS Presidential Address) in *Wesleyan Theological Journal*, vol. 44, no. 2 (Spring 2009): 58.

7. Kathleen Deyer Bolduc, *Autism and Alleluias* (Valley Forge, PA: Judson Press, 2010), 4.

8. Ibid., 5.

9. Ibid.

10. Ibid., 5-6.

11. Ibid., 6.

Chapter 14

1. Current and projected population statistics for the U.S. by race and Hispanic origin can be found on the U.S. Census Bureau site <http://www.census.gov/compendia/statab/2012/tables/>. Local statistics can also be searched on the site, although it must be remembered that the numbers may not reflect the extent of diversity because of underreporting.

2. Church of the Nazarene, "Our Mission: To Make Christlike Disciples in the Nations" <http://nazarene.org/ministries/superintendents/mission/display.html> (accessed March 14, 2013).

3. See Mark Mittelberg, Lee Strobel, and Bill Hybels, *Becoming a Contagious Christian: Communicating Your Faith in a Style That Fits You* (Grand Rapids: Zondervan, 2007).

4. The terms "multicultural," "cross-cultural," and "intercultural" are sometimes used interchangeably and sometimes distinguished. See "Defining Multicultural, Cross-cultural, and Intercultural," copyright 2011 by The United Church of Canada/L'Église Unie du Canada <http://www.united-church.ca/files/intercultural/multicultural-crosscultural-intercultural.pdf> (accessed December 14, 2011).

5. Vassel and Salguero eloquently express the contribution an outsider's theology can make to the dominant culture's limited perspective. See Sam Vassel and Gabriel Salguero, "The Immigrant Churches: Toward a Stranger's Theology," in *E Pluribus Unum: Challenges and Opportunities in Multicultural Ministry* (Kansas City: Beacon Hill Press of Kansas City, 2007).

6. The Spanish word *Palabra* completes the alliteration.

7. John Wesley, "Of the Church" <http://wesley.nnu.edu/john-wesley/the-sermons-of-john-wesley-1872-edition/>.

8. During these forty years all ministry, my (Mario) wife and I participated and witnessed the organization of many new districts, saw the membership of the MAC Region increased from 40,000 to 126,000 members, many new local churches were organized, and as well hundreds of pastors and missionaries were prepared and deployed to different world areas. It was a great privilege to experience firsthand the many changes theological education and the church in general went through during all of these years of ministry.

9. See David A. Livermore's detailed discussion of the implications of the iceberg metaphor in *Cultural Intelligence: Improving Your CQ to Engage Our Multicultural World* (Grand Rapids: Baker Academic, 2009).

10. It is important to note that the inclusive church may not always be the best option. Some argue that in recognition that the American melting pot is more like a salad bowl, immigrant-specific churches may be better. They can serve as places of refuge and community development especially for first-genera-

tion immigrants. See Oliver Phillips, "Who Moved My Church? Responding to the Changing Ethnic Landscape," in *E Pluribus Unum*.

11. Wesley, "Of the Church."

Chapter 15

1. The City of Oklahoma City, "Geographic Information Services" <http://www.okc.gov/info_tech/gis/index.html> (accessed March 22, 2013).

LAYING THE FOUNDATION

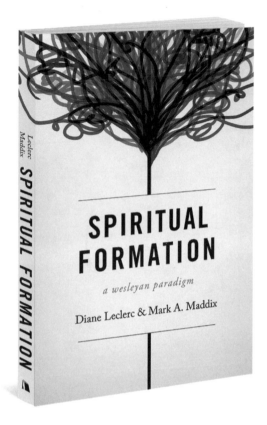

There is an increased interest in spirituality in our world lately.
People have a deep hunger and thirst for the transcendent.

In *Spiritual Formation,* Maddix and Leclerc provide a definition
of Christian spiritual formation within the Wesleyan paradigm
and assist faithful disciples in deepening their relationship
with Jesus Christ. The book focuses on how people can grow
in Christlikeness by participating in Scripture reading,
the sacraments, and other spiritual disciplines.

Spiritual Formation
By Diane Leclerc & Mark A. Maddix
ISBN: 978-0-8341-2613-8

BEACON HILL PRESS
OF KANSAS CITY
Available online at BeaconHillBooks.com